THE
PRICE
OF
PARADISE

EDITOR
Randall W. Roth

TECHNICAL EDITORS
James Mak
Jack P. Suyderhoud

MUTUAL PUBLISHING

Design
Michael Horton Design
Graphs
Bryant Fukutomi
Cover layout
John Roth

LCC #92-085480

First Printing September 1992
Second Printing November 1992
Third Printing February 1993
Fourth Printing January 1994

ISBN # I-56647-016-1

Mutual Publishing
1127 11th Avenue
Honolulu, Hawaii 96816
Telephone (808) 732-1709
Fax (808) 734-4094

Printed in Australia

ACKNOWLEDGMENTS

Jim Mak's title as Technical Editor doesn't do him justice. He helped to outline this book, select authors, review drafts for technical accuracy, and provide support to everyone involved in the project. Without Jim, there would not have been a book.

Jack Suyderhoud, initially one of many authors, ended up contributing in a dozen different ways. There might have been a book without Jack, but it would not have been nearly so accurate, complete or polished.

The authors were great about submitting their drafts on time and following guidelines. A few discounted my request to "avoid cliches like the plague," but all took seriously the one about avoiding dullness—the "D" word.

The *Honolulu Advertiser*'s Dick Adair and *Honolulu Star-Bulletin*'s Corky Trinidad allowed us to use their political cartoons, and even created some just for the book. Working with them was an absolute treat.

Joanne Punu, Larry Foster, Miki Okumura and Anita Lo helped greatly with editing. When they finally liked a chapter, I knew we had a winner.

Bennett Hymer of Mutual Publishing was a gift from above. His academic background (Ph.D. in Economics from Northwestern) was ideally suited to this book and his "can do" approach assured timely publication as well as high quality.

Jill Center of Strategic Communications provided priceless guidance in promoting the book, and she did it *pro bono*. With her help, we grew a lot more confident about reaching a broad cross section of Hawaii audiences.

Steven Gold, Director of the Center for the Study of States, at the Rockefeller Institute of Government, shared his considerable expertise, just as he has in past years on behalf of Hawaii State Tax Review Commissions. John Behrens of the Advisory Commission on Intergovernmental Relations also provided important input.

Jane Takata lent a valuable helping hand when deadlines loomed; Stuart Lillico's professional copy editing was humbling but much appreciated; Michael Horton worked magic in designing the book;

Bryant Fukutomi gave dimension to our data with his nifty graphs; and, John Roth's clever cover-layout fit the book perfectly.

Many individuals expressed interest and gave support along the way. *Hawaii Business* magazine's Diane Chang, *Hawaii Investor* magazine's Bill Wood, The *Honolulu Advertiser*'s Ann Harpham, *Honolulu Star-Bulletin*'s Bud Smyser and recently-retired state statistician Bob Schmitt were especially helpful.

I cannot say enough about the contribution of Helen Shikina. Besides being the world's greatest secretary, she has a knack for providing encouragement exactly when it is needed.

A number of friends reviewed the first draft of this book. Their comments (especially having to do with the "D" word) were a godsend. Thank you Dave, Deborah, Frieda, Gail, Iris, Laura, Lyle and Susie!

My wife, Susie, and the kids, Cassie, Wally, John and Tom, were more supportive than I thought possible. Their enthusiasm for the project assured its completion, if not its success.

This book is dedicated to the memory of Richard Pollock, professor of economics at the University of Hawaii who died in early 1992 at the peak of his career. Dick had been involved with this project from the beginning and his death left a void that never really was filled. The authors and I like to believe that Dick would be proud of the final product.

Randall W. Roth, Editor
July 1992

TABLE OF CONTENTS

INTRODUCTION

"Lucky you live Hawaii!" How long has it been since you last heard that? Unless it was a while back, it might have been tinged with sarcasm. A growing number of residents are less than convinced they're living in paradise.

My wife and I love Hawaii, but there is much that concerns us. We wonder if our children will settle here. Surely their chances of getting a job with a future and owning a home are better on the Mainland. It distresses us to picture our children—and, perhaps, grandchildren as well—living thousands of miles away.

We worry that Hawaii's entire economy is held aloft by a single thread called tourism. Recall, if you will, the effect on our local economy of the 1985 United Airlines strike, Operation Desert Storm, and the 1991-1992 national recession. If something goes wrong with Hawaii's tourism, will the entire economy shut down?

Taxes are high, the cost of living is even higher, and, when dealing with government, who you know seems to make more difference than it should. Housing is a problem, water seems scarce, public schools need more than just additional funding, and the population keeps growing (and aging).

Yet, everyone who worked on this book shares a love of Hawaii—what it has been and what it can be. We believe that no problem is too big if people care enough to work toward a long-term solution. This book is more interesting and educational than it is comforting. It probably won't make you feel better about living in Hawaii, but it will give you a clearer understanding of underlying problems—the first step toward doing something about them.

Economic focus. Hawaii's high cost of living has many residents wondering if life here is still worth the price. Certainly there's more to "quality of life" than just dollars and cents, but one must start somewhere in answering the question posed by this book's subtitle. I am hopeful that environmentalists, sociologists, moral philosophers and experts from other fields will continue and expand the dialogue.

Most of the authors are economists; the others are journalists, lawyers, an educator's educator and a demographer. Economists generally believe (1) efficiency is good, (2) government, while necessary, tends to be inefficient and too big, and (3) the long run is more

3

important than the short run. This is reflected in their chapters.

This book is intended to provoke thought and discussion. If you disagree with an author's bottom line, that isn't a problem. Articulate clearly your contrary position and the community will benefit. Informed dialogue is essential to a well-functioning democracy.

Role of government. Speaking of democracy, a thread running throughout the book is inquiry into the proper role of government. Government in Hawaii is uniquely pervasive; it affects all of us every day and in countless ways. Only in Hawaii, for example, have state and county governments virtually forced private developers out of business and then "saved the day" by arranging for the construction of thousands of homes. Consider also the State's "A+" program that provides inexpensive after-school child care. Normally, state and county governments are content to regulate businesses; here they compete with them.

The chapter titles read like a list of current events, but they are more than that. They represent challenges that never really go away. Hawaii's people were wrestling with variations a generation ago, and our children (if they are able to remain here) surely will be confronted with their own versions.

A group of chapters talk about taxes—maybe not the sexiest topic in the world, but one every citizen should understand. Keep in mind Deep Throat's priceless tip that led to the unraveling of the Watergate conspiracy: "Follow the money." It is not always simple—as you will find, for example, when you read how the legislature uses "smoke and mirrors" to hide the true level of government spending—but it is rewarding.

Short and nontechnical. Woodrow Wilson used to say he could give an excellent two-hour speech with no preparation, but a good ten-minute talk would require hours to prepare. One of the authors shared this anecdote upon hearing that each chapter had to come in either of two sizes ... short or shorter. The challenge was magnified by the instruction that each chapter had to be understandable to nonexperts.

For the same reason that prize fighters try not to lead with their chins, experts don't like to publish short nontechnical pieces. Without doubt, this book will be "nitpicked" by people who don't like its bottom-line conclusions. That's fine as long as critics go on to provide a clear explanation of their own positions. Your job is to insist that they do.

Our authors have taken this first step toward lively, informed dialogue as a service to the community. Neither I nor any of them will pocket a penny. Profits, if any, will go to local charities.

Are we lucky to be living in Hawaii? Only you can answer that for yourself. All of us, however, will answer it for our children and for their children. We inherited paradise; let's not let it die.

Randall W. Roth, Editor

CHAPTER 1

HAWAII'S COMPETITIVENESS

DAVID McCLAIN

Henry A. Walker, Jr. Distinguished Professor
of Business Enterprise and Financial Economics & Institutions
College of Business Administration
University of Hawaii

"What can Hawaii do to stay competitive in the world market and keep its economy strong?"

In today's global economy, every state is asking this question with more and more urgency. To their credit, Hawaii state and local officials have been concerned with economic development and Hawaii's competitiveness for a long time. Their main theme has been the idea of diversifying the economy away from its tourism base—natural enough, given our substantial dependence on this industry.

High-tech industries have been a particular target, but success has been elusive. While no one can deny the attractiveness of these high-wage, environmentally-friendly industries, every other state is trying the same thing. Hawaii faces tough competition, particularly from the more established areas such as Silicon Valley, Route 128 near Boston, the North Carolina Research Triangle, and Austin, Texas.

Moreover, this diversification approach, viewed as part of the state's economic development strategy, increasingly is out of step with the strategies followed by successful global corporations and developing countries today. While Hawaii is neither a company nor a country, state officials should learn what they can from others' experiences.

An outdated notion. In corporate strategy, diversification for its own sake is an outdated concept. The wave of corporate diversification so much in vogue in the late 1960s and early 1970s produced very few results. Managing businesses with unrelated component parts simply proved too hard and too unrewarding for shareholders.

The only corporate diversification still recommended is into a field related to the core business. A local example of this is PRI's decision to sell gasoline at retail through its Gas Express outlets. Such a strategic thrust, if carried off artfully, can indeed add value because management brings something to the party (its core-business acumen) and because the potential for *synergy* between the core business and a related business is high.

A similar change in thinking about diversification has taken place in many countries. During the 1960s and 1970s, every nation with a dominant single export product (for example, Chile and copper) wanted to diversify so as to buffer its economy from wide swings in prices and demand. Usually, these efforts failed. Some simply weren't attractive places to do business. They tended to have a large public sector—that is, government involvement in business. Perhaps this public sector had grown initially to help absorb the risk in promoting the special export. Subsequently, through bureaucratic dynamics, it had become a "black hole," draining the country's economy of its entrepreneurial energy.

Indeed, in many developing nations an unhealthy symbiosis occurred in which entrenched elites used the public sector to reinforce their political and economic power. Under such circumstances, diversification couldn't possibly succeed. What business would be attracted by such a "statist" economic climate?

During the debt crises of the 1980s, many countries realized that they had to shift their focus to doing better what they already were doing well, and creating a fertile environment in which new businesses could grow.

In a fertile economic environment, industries feed on and reinforce each other *synergistically* (there's that word again!), to produce what Michael Porter of the Harvard Business School calls sustainable competitive advantage. Porter suggests that four interdependent forces—a diamond—influence a nation's (or a state's) international competitiveness and its economic fertility. I like to extend the diamond image to baseball:

- At first base are the end market, or demand, conditions—the market size and the sophistication and preferences of consumers.
- At second base are the sophistication and the degree of rivalry in the domestic market. Firms that have had to live by their wits in a domestic market will do better in foreign markets.
- At third base are production factors—the supply of land, skilled labor, capital and the like.
- Finally, at home plate is the constellation of related and supporting industries. In today's global economy, production is so complex and specialized that a country or state needs a "critical mass" of related industries to support competitiveness.

Porter adds two "outside" influences: government (the umpire, to stick with our baseball analogy) and "chance." Either can affect any of the points of the diamond, for good or ill.

Hawaii's two diamonds. Hawaii really has two diamonds—one for the travel industry and one for the rest of the economy. Hawaii's tourism diamond is competitive, vibrant and mutually reinforcing. On the demand side, the customers are sophisticated and world class, the potential market is large, and Hawaii enjoys the benefits of a diversified clientele in Asia and in America.

As for supply, Hawaii's unique environment is a precious asset and America's political stability means that capital can flow into the islands freely. Related and supporting industries include the University of Hawaii's School of Travel Industry Management and its College of Languages, Linguistics and Literature (one of only three U.S. National Resource Centers for the Study of Foreign Language), as well as an entire nexus of travel-related firms, including the airlines and an excellent telecommunications network.

Competition in the travel and tourism industry in Hawaii is

vigorous; government, through the Hawaii Visitors' Bureau and other means, plays a supporting role.

This is not to say the travel and tourism industry is immune from business cycles in America or Japan, or from overbuilding, as has occurred on the neighbor islands. But the travel and tourism diamond, most would agree, is relatively healthy.

The rest of Hawaii's economy is another matter. Land is scarce and skilled labor is in short supply. The local market of 1.1 million people is not as sophisticated as those in major cities of Asia or the West, and those markets, in turn, are a long way away. Related and supporting industries for anything but travel and tourism are not world class, nor is competition at the same level of intensity as it is at other points around the Pacific Rim.

Because the state's natural beauty is such a remarkable asset, government has a special role in Hawaii. One would expect regulation's hand to be a bit heavier here. In fact, however, it goes well beyond the reasonable. There is really no excuse for the bureaucratic impediments that have pushed our housing prices and business costs so high. Cooper and Daws' *Land and Power in Hawaii* is among studies reporting that those in government have not always succeeded in separating private from public interest. The elite from our former plantation-based economy has been replaced by a new elite based in politics and real estate.

Competition is not encouraged. Government has done little to encourage competition. When the prospect for more competition in the local air market came up in 1991, in the form of interisland service by United Airlines, the immediate reaction of elected officials was to warn the prospective intruder away. But protection of local companies, in the name of protecting local consumers, could in fact be a smoke screen to help insiders hold their economic and political power.

In fact, the one-export-commodity developing country model, with an overdeveloped public sector that adversely affects entrepreneurial activity and an entrenched elite trying to maintain its privileges, has uncomfortable echoes in what we find in Hawaii today—and is one of the reasons Hawaii's competitive diamond (except for tourism) is so weak.

"So what should we do instead to insure appropriate development of Hawaii's economy?"

We need a strategy as sophisticated as the times in which we live. That means diversification, but in areas that build on our strength, that take advantage of the vibrant competitive diamond in our core business of tourism, and of its related and supporting industries. In essence, we're talking about "dancing with the one that brung you," instead of searching for a new partner.

It also means that we open our arms to outsiders who have something to share, and get rid of the mentality that puts "who you know" ahead of "what you know." Finally, it means convincing government that its proper role is umpiring business development, rather than trying to hit home runs as a player itself.

These basic principles have a couple of operational consequences. Hawaii should have—should have had five years ago—a convention center. Business travel is a natural adjunct to pleasure travel. The experiences of business travelers will do more to create Hawaii's image as a "Geneva of the Pacific" or "Capital of the Pacific" (with thanks for both of these to Bud Smyser) than all the advertising that money can buy.

Hawaii should shed its provincial outlook and build on its multicultural population. This includes promoting the state's educational institutions in Mainland and Asian markets and eliminating enrollment "caps" on outsiders.

Sensible diversification. Several other areas that build on Hawaii's strengths also make for sensible diversification. Health and sports-related industries fit well with the state's image as a universal health provider and a fitness mecca. For many reasons, golf courses are an almost ideal replacement for sugar, an industry that would have died here years ago had it not been for expensive federal "life support."

Certain types of scientific research and research-based activities, particularly those related to the oceans, the heavens, geology, biotechnology and tropical agriculture, fit naturally with the University of Hawaii's own distinctive competencies.

In both of these categories, Hawaii would be cooperating with two "chance" factors—demographic trends toward older, more health-conscious populations in industrial countries and a growing global concern about the environment.

As we focus on our core strengths, we must also take care to repair our weaknesses. Housing and education, the most prominent, receive plenty of attention in this book and elsewhere. I would only add that the industries mentioned above as good candidates for state promotional efforts generally require well-educated managers and workers. To attract these from the Mainland and Asia and to convince Hawaii's own sons and daughters to remain here, the quality of the state's education system and the affordability of its housing simply must improve. These two factors have become genuine bottlenecks to state economic expansion and growth.

Two other areas of weakness that need special attention are politics and the media.

Our political process is far too complacent. The state badly needs a genuine two-party system. Massachusetts was a one-party state. As a registered Democrat, I rather liked being a member of the party in power. But I have to admit that in 1988, when the recession hit Massachusetts with such vengeance, the state simply had not known the kind of healthy political debate that would have enabled it to cope with massive economic adversity.

Indeed, in the 1990 gubernatorial campaign the atmosphere was one of civic desperation, with a whiff of what Germany must have been like in the early 1930s. Candidates whose electability in normal times would have been questionable became their parties' nominees. In the end, the state turned to a wealthy Republican whose major theme was that he and his party weren't responsible for what had gone before.

Deja vu. As we see Hawaii's economy softening, I have a vague feeling of *deja vu.* I hope I'm wrong. And I hope we don't need a recession to revitalize the Republican Party. But I'm certain that a second vigorous and organized voice would improve the quality of our political decisions.

My second area of special concern is the media. With the exception of The *Honolulu Advertiser*'s James Dooley and *Hawaii Monitor*'s Ian Lind, the tradition of investigative journalism is underdeveloped in Hawaii, to put it kindly.

Journalists tell me that their local news is targeted at a mythical "Minnie Fukuda" who lives in Kalihi, is in her mid-50s, and worries mostly about the price of rice. But journalists need to keep Minnie's long-run interests in mind, too. Minnie and her descendants will be better served by a media that, by the energy of its reporting, forces consumers, businesses and government to compete more effectively in the marketplace of ideas. Such a setting will certainly produce government policies and laws more responsive to the state's needs.

In summary, we must build on our strengths. We must diversify, but in related, not unrelated areas. We also must adopt market-oriented reforms to create a more fertile field. Hawaii has fared well for a long time, but in many ways this has been despite governmental efforts rather than because of them. And the parochialism of an "old boys club" simply has to give way to a more enlightened global perspective if Hawaii is to compete effectively in an increasingly sophisticated world.

"BOY, PARKING IN SHOPPING CENTERS
IS REALLY GETTING TO BE A PROBLEM..."

CHAPTER 2

POPULATION SIZE

ROBERT W. GARDNER

Research Associate
Program on Population
East-West Center

"Can we limit the size of our population to its current level?"

On April 1, 1990, the date of the last census, 1,108,229 people were counted in Hawaii. This included 115,268 members of the armed forces and their dependents. It did not include tourists. The total was almost 44 percent higher than a generation earlier in 1970. That's a lot of people. But before we can reasonably conclude it is "too many," we have to determine the optimum population for the state.

About 20 years ago, Earl Babbie, a professor of sociology at the University of Hawaii, published "The Maximillion Report." In it Babbie looked at such dimensions of "quality of life" as ecological balance, health and safety, human freedom and dignity, cultural variety, economic variety, self-sufficiency and natural beauty. He then examined the effects on these areas of trends in personal income, government costs, crime rates, number of automobiles, agricultural self-sufficiency and recreation. He found evidence of a steady decline in the quality of life in Hawaii.

"Optimum" population. At the end of his booklet, Babbie concluded, "In many respects, we seem to have already exceeded our optimum population." He proposed that the state immediately estab-lish a population ceiling of one million and work to stay within that limit. Hence the term, maximillion.

Of course the goal was not established, and the million mark is history. If Babbie were writing today, he would probably come to the same conclusion he came to 20 years ago: population growth has been an important factor in the decline of the quality of life in Hawaii.

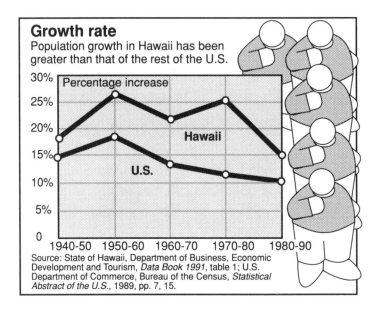

Growth rate
Population growth in Hawaii has been greater than that of the rest of the U.S.

Percentage increase

Hawaii

U.S.

Source: State of Hawaii, Department of Business, Economic Development and Tourism, *Data Book 1991*, table 1; U.S. Department of Commerce, Bureau of the Census, *Statistical Abstract of the U.S.*, 1989, pp. 7, 15.

Not everyone agreed with Babbie's conclusions then, and not everyone would agree now. Certain industries and interests, such as construction, depend on continual population growth. More gener-ally, population growth is often seen as a sign of economic and social well-being. "Stagnant" is usually used to describe places where the population is no longer growing.

As Babbie noted, "every reader will agree that there is *some* finite limit to the population which these islands can support with a reasonable quality

of life." Regardless of what one's chosen optimum is, then, at some point population growth must be stopped or quality of life will plummet.

So the answer to the question, "Are there too many people in Hawaii?" is, "It depends." But if growth continues, ultimately everyone must answer "Yes!"

Why population grows. Only two factors can possibly affect population growth: natural increase (the difference between the number of births and the number of deaths) and net migration (the difference between the number of migrants to and from the state).

Between 1970 and 1980, there were roughly 83,000 more births than deaths in the civilian population. Between 1980 and 1990, the difference dropped slightly to about 79,000. In the first of these two decades, natural increase accounted for approximately 44 percent of total civilian growth of 190,000. In the more recent decade, natural increase, while lower, accounted for almost 53 percent of our 149,000 civilian growth.

Net civilian migration between 1970 and 1980 was approximately 106,000; between 1980 and 1990 it was roughly 71,000. In the first decade, this amounted to almost 56 percent of total civilian growth, while in the second it was almost 48 percent.

The above figures show that population growth in recent decades has been fueled by both natural increase and net migration. Does this mean that, if we want to slow growth, we can "attack" on either or both fronts? Surprisingly, no.

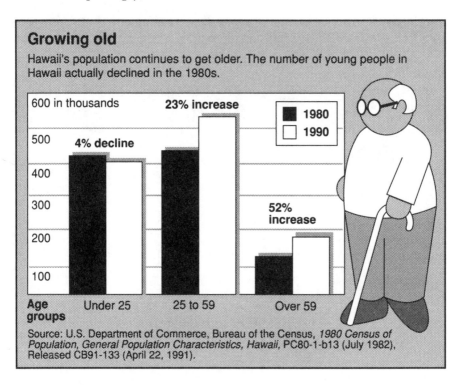

Growing old

Hawaii's population continues to get older. The number of young people in Hawaii actually declined in the 1980s.

Source: U.S. Department of Commerce, Bureau of the Census, *1980 Census of Population, General Population Characteristics, Hawaii*, PC80-1-b13 (July 1982), Released CB91-133 (April 22, 1991).

The surplus of births over deaths, although real, is misleading. Civilian women in Hawaii have been having children at a rate that, if continued, would result in a near balance of births and deaths. Births have outnumbered deaths because Hawaii still has a relatively young population, with a high proportion in the child-bearing ages. If current civilian fertility rates continue indefinitely (and if the population continues to "age"), natural increase will contribute less and less to Hawaii's growth.

Migration is main source. This would leave net migration as the most important source of population growth. The current balance is positive, but a number of people do leave the state (some of them undoubtedly because of the declining quality of life). In 1987 and 1988, for example, approximately 2.5 percent of the civilian population thought there was a good chance or almost a certainty of living elsewhere within one year.

Out-migration receives relatively little notice, however; attention usually focuses on the migrants from the Mainland ("in-migrants") and from abroad ("immigrants"). Immigrants who gave Hawaii as their intended residence for the five years 1986-1990 totaled more than 36,000, roughly half of the ten-year total net migration. Does this mean that our net migration is due to immigrants? No. Immigrants are a notoriously mobile group, and undoubtedly many moved on to the Mainland (or returned home), ultimately contributing nothing to net migration.

Other figures give us a different picture of the balance of immigrants and in-migrants. Data from U.S. Government surveys for the period 1981-1989 show that, of people living in Hawaii who had lived elsewhere one year earlier, usually about 80 percent had been in another state, only 20 percent in a different country. Almost exactly the same figures were obtained in 1985 about residence five years earlier. It thus appears that our migrants (the people here now who weren't here before) are predominantly from the Mainland.

These figures indicate that net migration was lower during the 1980s than the 1970s. Nevertheless, there is still substantial net migration to the state. If it continues, this will be the major factor in future population growth. This conclusion is bolstered when we consider that migrants often are young adults. Continued net migration might retard the "aging" of the population and thus keep the natural increase well above zero, in spite of relatively low fertility per woman.

Limit size? To limit the size of our population, we would have to affect natural increase or net migration. To affect natural increase, we would have to affect mortality or fertility. No one is about to suggest increasing mortality, so that leaves lowering fertility. But we have already seen that fertility in Hawaii is just about at the proverbial two-child-family "replacement" level and is unlikely to fall much.

Many people think we should limit migration into the state. This means either limiting in-migration from the Mainland, or limiting immigration from abroad, or both. It turns out that "we" (the state government) are pretty helpless when it comes to limiting migration of either kind, at least legally.

The U.S. Constitution guarantees the right to move freely among the states. It does not seem likely that any plea that Hawaii is a special case would receive much of a hearing. Similarly, the state cannot impose any restrictions on new in-migrants; a policy of not hiring newcomers in state jobs was declared unconstitutional 20 years ago.

We can't restrict immigration, either. In the nineteenth century the states were allowed different immigration rules, but the federal government has long since preempted the field. Hawaii can say nothing about the number of immigrants entering the state.

What about the "poor, unskilled aliens" who seem to dominate the immigrant flow to Hawaii? Why don't we keep them out? Well, we can't keep out any single class of immigrants anymore than we can keep out immigrants in general: it's a federal issue. True, the new (1991) U.S. immigration law places more emphasis on qualifications than did the preceding law, so that the mix of occupations and levels of training may change. On the other hand, most immigrants since 1965 have come to the United States under family reunification provisions of the law, and this promises to remain true. Besides, the "poor, unskilled aliens" provide much of the cheap labor for Hawaii's important tourist industry.

People move to Hawaii because of its attractions. Many of these attractions are the same ones that attract tourists. If the quality of life in these islands declines because of, among other things, population growth and its effects, the consequences might be fewer migrants and fewer tourists. At some point we might reach a balance with no net migration and essentially zero natural increase. However, if this is accomplished "naturally," Hawaii might be a far less pleasant place in which to live. And, as we have seen, it is not likely that we can reach zero growth "unnaturally" (through legislation), because our hands are tied. We are faced with the same dilemma that Babbie faced two decades ago, only with a much larger population.

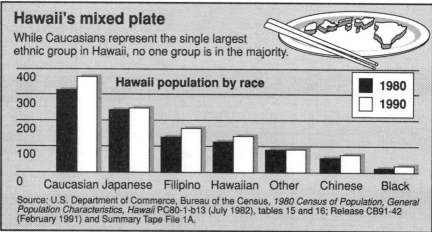

Hawaii's mixed plate

While Caucasians represent the single largest
ethnic group in Hawaii, no one group is in the majority.

Hawaii population by race

■ 1980
□ 1990

400
300
200
100
0

Caucasian Japanese Filipino Hawaiian Other Chinese Black

Source: U.S. Department of Commerce, Bureau of the Census, *1980 Census of Population, General
Population Characteristics, Hawaii* PC80-1-b13 (July 1982), tables 15 and 16; Release CB91-42
(February 1991) and Summary Tape File 1A.

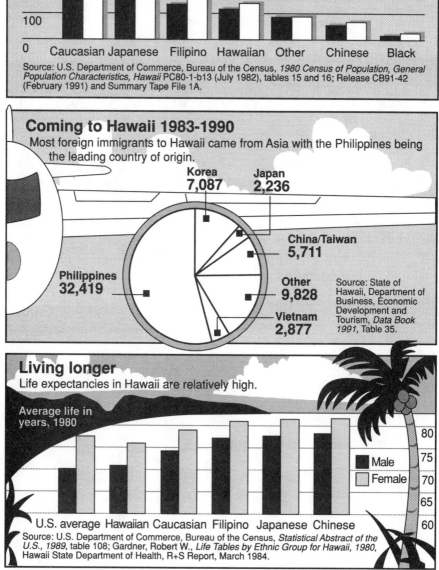

Coming to Hawaii 1983-1990

Most foreign immigrants to Hawaii came from Asia with the Philippines being
the leading country of origin.

Korea
7,087

Japan
2,236

China/Taiwan
5,711

Philippines
32,419

Other
9,828

Vietnam
2,877

Source: State of
Hawaii, Department of
Business, Economic
Development and
Tourism, *Data Book
1991*, Table 35.

Living longer

Life expectancies in Hawaii are relatively high.

Average life in
years, 1980

80
75
70
65
60

■ Male
□ Female

U.S. average Hawaiian Caucasian Filipino Japanese Chinese

Source: U.S. Department of Commerce, Bureau of the Census, *Statistical Abstract of the
U.S., 1989*, table 108; Gardner, Robert W., *Life Tables by Ethnic Group for Hawaii, 1980*,
Hawaii State Department of Health, R+S Report, March 1984.

CHAPTER 3

COST OF LIVING

LEROY O. LANEY
Vice President and Chief Economist
First Hawaiian Bank

"Why is the cost of living in Hawaii so high? Will it ever come down?"

Hawaii's cost of living ranks high on most people's list of complaints about our economy, and it heads many. Cost of living differences between Hawaii and the Mainland are indeed stunning—a "sticker shock" from which newcomers and long-time residents alike never really recover.

This is not a short-term aberration. To illustrate, let's consider a time frame well within the memory of most adult residents —1970 to 1990. The annual intermediate household dollar outlay for a four-person family on Oahu in 1970 was around 20 percent higher than the mainland average—enough to make the budget-minded blanch even then. As late as 1986 the outlay in Hawaii was still only 23 percent higher. Between 1986 and 1990, however, the difference grew to a staggering 34 percent.

Main culprit. Housing is the main culprit. Coldwell Banker does a survey each year comparing the cost of similar homes in 251 locations around the United States. The "subject home" and neighborhood are suitable for the "typical" corporate middle-management transferee. The 1992 price of a "subject home" in Honolulu—$594,750—was considerably above almost all of the other 250 locations. In most cases it was dramatically higher.

Price of "subject home" in
Coldwell Banker study
(partial list)

Albuquerque	$158,300
Anchorage	$165,700
Atlanta	$138,538
Austin	$149,250
Chicago-Lincoln Park	$387,833
Dallas	$131,000
Denver	$140,813
Honolulu	**$594,750**
Kansas City, KS	$107,883
Kansas City, MO	$172,500
Las Vegas	$139,981
Minneapolis	$168,107
Montreal	$102,343
Phoenix	$117,600
Pittsburgh	$142,000
Portland, OR	$147,833
St. Louis	$131,050
Salt Lake City	$136,967
San Jose	$380,825
Seattle	$174,750
Tampa	$125,100
Washington,D.C.-Inside Beltway	$318,625
Washington, D.C.-Outside Beltway	$197,550

The National Association of Realtors (NAR) uses a home affordability index to measure the degree to which a middle-income family can afford mortgage payments. A value of 100 means barely enough income to qualify for an 80 percent mortgage on a median-price home. The higher the index, the more affordable the housing. Honolulu's 1990 single-family home affordability index of 39.6 was lower than that of any of the 31 metropolitan areas studied. But in 1991 the index for Honolulu actually rose to 57.7. That lifted Honolulu off the bottom of the list, putting it at least ahead of the California cities.

So some relative progress occurred in 1991. The easing of speculative pressures associated with Japanese purchases caused an actual decline in average and median prices in Honolulu. This plus lower interest rates and continued rise in incomes helped to increase our affordability index.

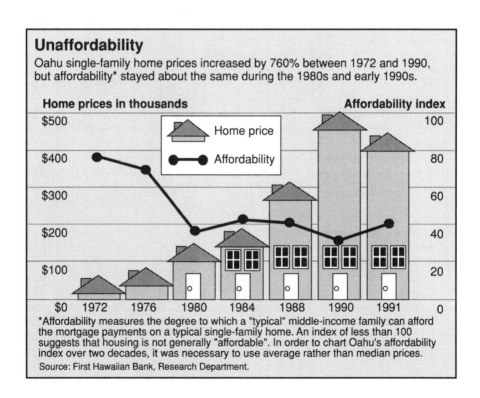

Unaffordability

Oahu single-family home prices increased by 760% between 1972 and 1990, but affordability* stayed about the same during the 1980s and early 1990s.

*Affordability measures the degree to which a "typical" middle-income family can afford the mortgage payments on a typical single-family home. An index of less than 100 suggests that housing is not generally "affordable". In order to chart Oahu's affordability index over two decades, it was necessary to use average rather than median prices.
Source: First Hawaiian Bank, Research Department.

Composite Affordability Index
(using metropolitan area median prices)

Metro area	1990	1991
Atlanta	123.7	128.5
Baltimore	100.1	97.6
Boston	65.9	64.9
Chicago	85.5	80.4
Cincinnati	115.7	118.9
Cleveland	116.4	115.8
Columbus	113.5	114.5
Dallas	114.2	123.6
Denver	118.6	123.0
Detroit	133.5	134.0
Honolulu	**39.6**	**57.7**
Houston	149.2	157.9
Indianapolis	120.0	127.0
Kansas City, MO/KS	122.8	122.8
Los Angeles	43.0	43.8
Louisville	134.8	136.7
Miami	89.7	91.1
Milwaukee	113.4	113.6
Minneapolis/St. Paul	121.6	129.5
New York	46.9	64.3
Philadelphia	89.6	93.5
Phoenix	109.2	117.2
Pittsburgh	122.1	124.1
Portland	103.3	102.5
Rochester	125.5	133.6
Salt Lake City	135.2	134.9
San Diego	51.2	49.4
San Francisco Bay	43.3	43.2
Seattle	68.2	72.2
St. Louis	131.7	129.6
Tampa	104.1	115.1
Washington, D.C.	88.4	90.9

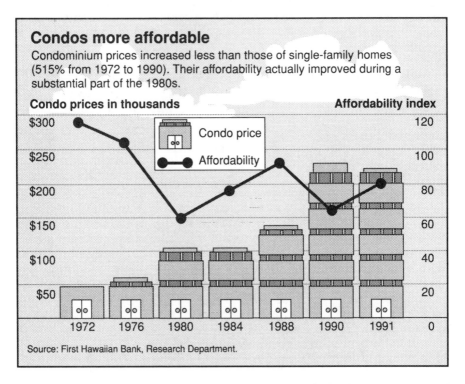

Condos more affordable

Condominium prices increased less than those of single-family homes (515% from 1972 to 1990). Their affordability actually improved during a substantial part of the 1980s.

Condo prices in thousands — **Affordability index**

Condo price
Affordability

| | 1972 | 1976 | 1980 | 1984 | 1988 | 1990 | 1991 |

Source: First Hawaiian Bank, Research Department.

In Hawaii, homeowners spend an unusually high percentage of their income on housing. How do they get mortgage loans? Many can do so only if joined by mothers, fathers, uncles, aunts or other reluctant but cooperative souls.

Other prices high, too. Food prices in Hawaii are about 30 percent higher than on the Mainland. Most people assume that this is primarily due to added transportation costs. However, trans-Pacific shipping cost is a relatively minor factor, perhaps adding no more than 5 percent to the retail price of food. A much bigger factor is the need for grocers to maintain bigger inventories—in some cases three times bigger—in order to keep items on the shelves at all times. Mainland stores closer to food sources can keep their inventories down and still keep the shelves full.

Like other businesses in Hawaii, food wholesalers and retailers pay far more for the use of land and buildings than do their counterparts on the Mainland. And, of course, Hawaii's 4 percent excise tax adds to the cost of food. Some just assume they are being gouged by food retailers, but excess profit doesn't seem to be the problem. Net profit margins in Hawaii are about 1.3 percent, roughly equal to what one finds on the Mainland.

The prices for other major consumer outlays—car prices, gasoline, parking and day care, for example, just to list a few—are also affected by some of the same factors. In fact, few categories of consumption expenditure in the islands are not influenced to some extent by scarce land, logistical difficulties and scarce labor that is in turn partly due to the high cost of living.

"FOR LOCALS-WE HAVE A COUPLE OF GREEN FEE FINANCING PLANS: PLAN A: 20% DOWN AND WEEKLY PAYMENTS AT 18% ..."

In addition to this list, however, at least one other aspect of Hawaii's high cost of living deserves mention. Personal income taxes are particularly burdensome here. In fact, when one compares the average four-person family budget on Oahu to urban U.S. averages, it is the tax category here that outstrips the Mainland the most. Total personal income taxes were almost 62 percent higher in Hawaii in 1981; by 1990, that had risen to 76 percent higher.

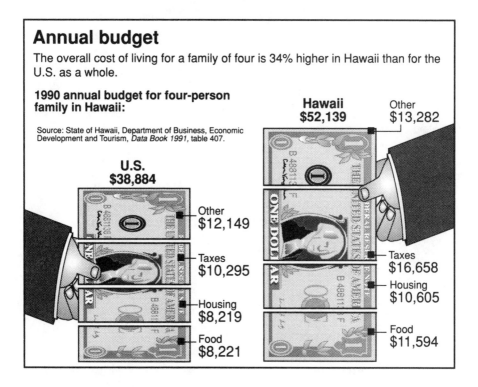

Annual budget

The overall cost of living for a family of four is 34% higher in Hawaii than for the U.S. as a whole.

1990 annual budget for four-person family in Hawaii:

Source: State of Hawaii, Department of Business, Economic Development and Tourism, *Data Book 1991*, table 407.

U.S.
$38,884

Other
$12,149

Taxes
$10,295

Housing
$8,219

Food
$8,221

Hawaii
$52,139

Other
$13,282

Taxes
$16,658

Housing
$10,605

Food
$11,594

Change possible? Given that many of us have chosen to live in Hawaii, what can and cannot be changed in this painful situation?

First, the inevitable. Hawaii, like many isolated island economies, long has had high living costs. Land will always be high, and higher land costs affect not only the cost of living but of doing business as well. These higher business costs inevitably get paid by consumers.

It is harder to understand other aspects of the local cost of living. For example, some things actually produced locally carry a higher retail price in Hawaii than elsewhere.

Ever wonder why pineapple canned in Honolulu costs more in Hawaii than on the Mainland? To answer this frequently asked question, we must consider demand as well as supply. As for demand, "substitutes" like oranges and chocolate, for example, may cost so much they drive up the price of pineapples. On the supply side, retailers in Hawaii traditionally have chosen to compete primarily on levels other than price. This is not surprising in that they have a limited market and a more-or-less "captive" consumer. One consequence is that our retailers often are not very efficient, and prices tend to reflect that.

Blame for the primary contributor to the high cost of living—housing—has been leveled at foreign speculation, a strong economy and a growing population. Yet it is on the supply side that we find the real villain. Supply of new housing—the only viable way housing prices can be reduced significantly—is restricted by local land-use policies and a prolonged development process. This important topic receives extensive attention elsewhere in this book.

Negative consequences. High cost of living has far-reaching effects on Hawaii's economy. In-migration to this otherwise desirable location with plenty of jobs is discouraged, contributing to the state's chronic labor shortage. Out-migration, on which statistics are poor, also has become a serious problem. Those leaving are not just younger workers who can't make ends meet and retirees who can no longer afford to live here. People at midcareer with good jobs find it attractive to sell their Hawaii home and move to the Mainland where homes and other living costs are lower.

High land and other prices also are a major hurdle to diversification of Hawaii's tourism-dependent economy. Hawaii can thank its uniqueness as a tourism destination for the survival and health of its visitor industry. Many competitor destinations are lower priced and closer to their markets to boot. But other sectors of the economy such as film making and many high-tech applications are quite difficult to develop because of high costs. Thus, the diversification that would be hard for any economy as small and specialized as ours becomes an increasingly elusive goal as costs accelerate.

The perception that only the wealthy find it easy to live in Hawaii, combined with the fact that job creation is mainly of a lower income variety, leads to the conjecture that Hawaii is gaining untrained lower-income workers and losing the better educated, trained middle class. We fear a continuing "brain drain" of major proportions in the middle-income ranks, while rich and poor are left to stare at each other across the fence. Obviously, few things are more divisive in an economy, as increasing social tensions make any kind of consensus harder to achieve.

Research by First Hawaiian Bank, using federal income tax return data for Hawaii, shows income distribution got steadily more equal from about 1929 to 1959. Since then, however, it has become consistently less equal. Today, Hawaii ranks 32 on the list of the 50 states in the equality of income among its residents.

Though it is small comfort, there is some evidence that the distribution of income in Hawaii is on a trend similar to the Mainland. In fact, Hawaii's income distribution was slightly less equal than the nation's in 1970, but today it is barely more equal. Transition to a service economy is one reason for trends toward more unequal distribution of income at the national as well as the state level.

The bright side? Clearly, life in paradise does have its price. But economists generally embrace relative prices as a means to allocate scarce resources. Good things should and do cost more, so it is reasonable that living in Hawaii with its strong economy and beautiful environment might be more expensive than living elsewhere. High prices ration this favorable environment to those willing to pay those prices. In doing so, they preserve it.

If prices in Hawaii were in line with less attractive places, we would have more in-migration and less out-migration. More people, cars and effluents would make our environment permanently less desirable. From this perspective, who can say existing prices in Hawaii are "too high"? It may be trite to claim it, and the answer will not satisfy those of us who are trying to remain in the face of difficult odds, but from a broader perspective prices do their job.

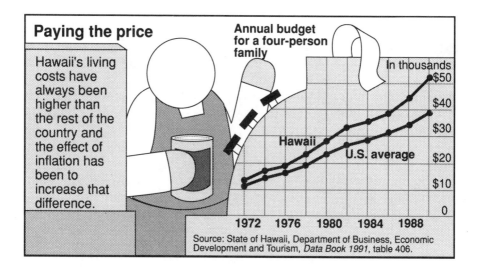

Paying the price

Hawaii's living costs have always been higher than the rest of the country and the effect of inflation has been to increase that difference.

Annual budget for a four-person family

In thousands

Hawaii

U.S. average

$50
$40
$30
$20
$10
0

1972 1976 1980 1984 1988

Source: State of Hawaii, Department of Business, Economic Development and Tourism, *Data Book 1991*, table 406.

CHAPTER 4

FOREIGN INVESTMENT

JAMES MAK
Professor of Economics
University of Hawaii

MARCIA Y. SAKAI
Assistant Professor
Business Administration and Economics Division
University of Hawaii at Hilo

"Is foreign investment good or bad for Hawaii?"

A 1988 statewide survey revealed that 59 percent of our residents opposed more **foreign** investment in Hawaii. Only 33 percent favored encouraging such investment. A year later, 60 percent of a different group were against additional **Japanese** investments here.

Why would the people of Hawaii be opposed to foreign investment in general, and to Japanese investment in particular? After all, mainland states roll out the red carpet at a moment's notice for a prospective investor (foreign or otherwise). It's not as though outside investors are new to Hawaii. They built our sugar industry 150 years ago and our pineapple industry nearly 100 years ago. Perhaps the opposition has something to do with the level of investment.

According to the Department of Business, Economic Development & Tourism's 1991 *Data Book*, the actual amount of foreign investment in Hawaii is staggering. For example, foreign investors now own over half of the office space in downtown Honolulu, almost two-thirds of all hotel rooms in the state and almost 9 percent of our agricultural property (second highest percentage in the nation, way above the national average of 1.1 percent).

Mainly Japanese. In Hawaii, "foreign investment" and "Japanese investment" are virtually synonymous. A 1991 study by Kenneth Leventhal & Company, a national accounting firm, showed that Japanese put $7.3 billion into Hawaiian real estate in 1989 and 1990 alone. Their 1990 purchases constituted 98 percent of all foreign investment in Hawaii that year. By the end of 1990, Japanese investment was nearly six times greater than all other foreign investments combined. Land and tourism industry assets constitute the bulk of local wealth. Interestingly, 95 percent of Japanese investment has been in these two categories.

Outside investment has deeply affected us in ways that cannot be quantified. Perhaps Governor John Waihee summed it up best when he commented, "Hawaii's residents are experiencing a sense of loss ... of their land to others and, more importantly, loss of control."

Before addressing this "sense of loss," it's appropriate to consider the economic effects of foreign investment.

There are two kinds. One is "new investment," where a foreign investor builds, for example, a new hotel. Another is a "takeover," as when a foreign investor buys an existing hotel. New investment creates jobs, pushes wage levels up, increases the price of land and generates additional tax revenue. This is all good if you are an owner of investment land (the value of which has just increased), a worker (whose services are now in greater demand and more valuable) and/or a taxpayer looking for someone to help pay the costs of government. Competitors, such as owners of existing hotels, may be worse off, but the community will enjoy higher total income.

People who do not own investment land or work in the hotel business may think they personally are not benefitted by this sort of foreign investment, but they are wrong. There is a very important "ripple effect" as direct beneficiaries spend those new dollars locally and as increased tax revenues finance more and better services for all residents.

The case for foreign "takeover investment" is much more complicated. The bottom line, however, depends on the seller's disposition of
the sale proceeds, the buyer's willingness to invest in improving the
purchased asset, and the buyer's ability to manage that asset better than
it was managed by the seller. The Japanese, in particular, often improve
assets acquired in takeovers. The $50 million renovation of Hawaii's
oldest hotel, the Moana Surfrider, is one example. In such instances,
foreign purchases result in net benefits to residents.

Net gain. Most people in Hawaii agree that, on balance, and
measured in dollars and cents, both "new" and "takeover" foreign
investments benefit residents. Opposition to foreign investment is
largely based on the perceived negative social impact.

A lot of the unfriendliness (hostility?) directed toward Japanese
investors is the result of their purchases of homes during the late 1980s
and early 1990s. In 1990 alone, they spent an estimated $400 million
on residential property. This is a tremendous amount (given Hawaii's
small size) and undoubtedly would have had a significant impact on
some neighborhoods, even if the buyers had paid only "market value."
The University of Hawaii Real Estate Research and Education Center
found that in one particularly popular neighborhood (Kahala), Japanese buyers paid a 21 percent premium over market value.

Between 1987 and 1990, the median price of a single-family home
on Oahu rose from $185,000 to $352,000—an increase of 90 percent
in just three years. People locked out of the inflated home market
blamed Japanese investors. Many existing homeowners were just as
upset when assessed values of their homes increased substantially as a
result of the high prices. These homeowners assumed (usually correctly) that a substantially higher assessed value meant a higher
property tax.

One Japanese businessman, Genshiro Kawamoto, made headlines
by offering cash for homes (many of which were not even up for sale)
from the back seat of his limousine. He acquired 100 East Honolulu
properties very quickly that way and indicated a goal of up to 1,000. His
approach hardly endeared him to locals struggling to achieve their
American dream.

Many of the 100 houses bought by Kawamoto were rented back to
the sellers, so the neighborhoods were not necessarily altered. But

others were bought for occasional use, for corporate retreats or simply for short-term speculation. These transactions often changed the character of a neighborhood. Houses would sit empty for months or be used by "transients" who had no interest in assimilating into the community. Some fell into disrepair and became eyesores.

Someone to blame. Because Japanese purchases occurred when housing was especially tight and prices were shooting up, many residents blamed both conditions on them. Housing experts, however, attributed both largely to Hawaii's then-booming economy. Local politicians, meanwhile, simply sat back, thankful that their constituents had someone else to blame.

The truth is that Japanese investors were a significant short-term factor in Hawaii's housing problems, but probably a minor factor in the long run. Their buying binge was the result of a confluence of factors unlikely to be seen again soon. The yen had virtually doubled in value in relationship to the dollar, interest rates in Japan were amazingly low (5 to 6 percent), Tokyo banks were basing loans on the value of the collateral with little concern about the purchased asset's ability to generate cash flow, land and stock prices in Japan were phenomenally high, and investment overseas was being encouraged by the Japanese government. All in all, this was an amazing combination. As Japanese investors retreat during the 1990s, housing prices may fall, but not dramatically (except, of course, for the multimillion-dollar mansions built with only free-spending Japanese in mind).

Other reasons explain some of the anti-Japanese investment sentiment. There is considerable concern about discriminatory hiring policies. An early 1970s study confirmed that Japanese businesses in Hawaii mainly hired Japanese nationals and Japanese-Americans. There also is concern that women find it difficult to ascend the Japanese corporate ladder. Local business owners feel that Japanese preference to do business with each other will lock them out as suppliers. These are legitimate concerns against which we must guard.

Japanese businesses are also often accused of being reluctant to participate in community affairs or to contribute to charities. Perhaps this can be blamed on unfamiliarity with local customs. Here we have a responsibility to educate newcomers to our way of doing business. Yoshiharu Satoh, chief executive officer and chairman of the Central

Pacific Bank in Honolulu, has led the way in educating other Japanese about community expectations. In short, both sides need to work harder to maximize the economic benefits and to minimize the social costs of foreign investment in Hawaii.

Loss of control? Finally, does Japanese investment in Hawaii translate sooner or later into a loss of control over our own future? It could, if we let it. All else remaining the same, there is no question that it would be better if residents of Hawaii owned these assets, rather than outsiders, whether from Japan, Australia, Taiwan, Canada or California. That's not possible, however, at least not if we want to maintain our current standard of living.

Fortunately, while they may wield considerable economic clout in Hawaii, Japanese investors (so far) haven't shown much interest in wielding political influence. And we should try to keep it that way.

If anything, it is the Japanese who have submitted themselves to *our* control! How would you like to have billions of dollars sunk in a faraway place whose residents make all the rules? You wouldn't, unless you trusted those residents. Indeed, by the sheer volume of their investments in Hawaii, Japanese have shown a lot of confidence in our sense of fair play.

Attitudes toward Japanese investments often change with economic and political conditions. Many residents hold out welcome signs when times are bad, then complain about foreign involvement when times are good. Remember, we cannot turn foreign investment on and off like a faucet. Mixed signals will only discourage beneficial investments. Any damage done during the good times likely will be felt later, with negative economic consequences for us.

Are foreign investments good or bad for Hawaii? There is no simple answer. But if we are protective of our interests while dealing fairly with theirs, everyone can come out ahead. We can then say, "Lucky they invest Hawaii."

CHAPTER 5

INTERISLAND FAIRNESS

LOWELL L. KALAPA
President
Tax Foundation of Hawaii

"Do neighbor islanders get their fair share of benefits from the State?"

State government in Hawaii has long dominated the counties. Among other things, this has resulted in an "overfinanced" state and "underfinanced" counties, at least by mainland standards. This explains the annual ritual of mayors, tin plates in hand, begging for handouts from the Honolulu-based state government. The City and County of Honolulu always gets the largest handout—to be expected when almost all of the state's economic activity takes place there. But given recent surges in the population and amount of state taxes generated by activity outside Honolulu, it's easy to see why neighbor island residents would eye Honolulu's big slice and wonder if their county is getting a "fair share" of the state pie.

Until the early 1970s the neighbor islands were almost exclusively rural, with no industry to speak of other than sugar or pineapple. With this minimal economic base, it was a given that they needed more services from the State than their economies could pay for. Generally speaking, the State was generous, softening the adverse effect of a weak economic base and sparing residents the ills of economic development. All in all, it was a comfortable arrangement for neighbor islanders.

With the tourism boom, however, industrial bases broadened. Population and business activity increased dramatically, as did the neighbor islands' contribution to state revenues. At the same time, they started to notice traffic congestion, pollution, housing shortages and other by-products of progress.

Demanding an accounting. As a result, neighbor island residents have begun to demand some sort of accounting for what they contribute in state taxes, relative to the grants and services they receive. Although state revenues are derived from a variety of taxes, including income taxes, the focus has largely been on the 4 percent general excise tax. However, taxpayers doing business in more than one county would file their returns and pay their taxes in Honolulu. This "unified reporting" made it impossible to determine how much resulted from economic activity on each neighbor island. In 1990, unified reporting was repealed.

Unfortunately, allocation on a county-by-county basis still proved to be difficult. Data collected for 1991, the first year this new reporting requirement was in effect, were inaccurate and inconclusive.

On the other hand, the hotel-room tax is tied to the gross rental income of each specific property, so county-by-county reports are quite accurate. Although there have been slight variations in the percentage of county-by-county collections of this tax since it was first imposed in 1987, the slices have remained relatively constant. About 60 percent of the hotel-room tax is collected in Honolulu, 23 percent on Maui, 9 percent on Hawaii and 8 percent on Kauai.

The 1990 legislature decided to give the counties 95 percent of all future hotel-room taxes, retaining 5 percent for the cost of collection and administration. However, rather than return these funds to the counties on the basis of where the tax was generated, the legislature established an arbitrary schedule of percentage distribution with Honolulu receiving 44.1 percent instead of 60 percent, Maui 22.8 percent, Hawaii 18.6 percent and Kauai 14.5 percent. Based on this statutory division of the spoils, Honolulu receives less than its "fair share" of hotel-room taxes. Hawaii and Kauai counties appear to be the big winners.

One could argue that the allocation of hotel-room taxes to the counties should be based on where the money is needed rather than where it was collected. But the formula used in the now-terminated federal revenue-sharing program—a formula generally acclaimed as one of the best ever implemented—suggests that a proper distribution of state funds to the counties would have been 69.1 percent to Honolulu, 9.9 percent to Maui, 14.9 percent to Hawaii and 6.1 percent to Kauai.

But what about other state tax collections? Are the neighbor islands getting their fair share of them?

Consultant report. The Hawaii State Tax Review Commission sought assistance in 1989 from the independent Washington, D.C.-based U.S. Advisory Commission on Intergovernmental Relations (ACIR) on this question. While the ACIR allocation of revenues and expenditures may not be the absolute last word on who benefits and who pays, it is the only known attempt to address this issue in a complete and systematic fashion.

Analyzing revenue and expenditure data for fiscal 1987, the ACIR found that, based on their allocations, Big Island residents were the big winners, receiving $670 more per capita in state-provided services than they contributed in state taxes. Running a not-too-distant second were Kauai islanders who received $552 more per capita in state services than they paid in state taxes. Farther back in third position, Maui residents were $108 to the good.

Honolulu fell below the break-even line, with residents paying $114 more than they received from the State. While it could be argued that certain cost efficiencies can be achieved with delivery of state services to a larger population base, the fact cannot be ignored that Honolulu subsidizes the delivery of those same services to neighbor island residents.

The ACIR also examined how well the counties had tapped their own sources of revenue, the idea being that neighbor islands deserve a handout only if they already are making the most of their taxing capacity.

Maui County's capacity to finance its own public services was $12.8 million or 19 percent above average. Kauai's excess capacity was $4.6 million, 14 percent above average. In other words, these two counties (relative to the other two) were able to finance service at levels substantially above average or could finance average service levels with below-average user fees and/or property tax rates. The ACIR found that Maui was in such a strong fiscal position that it could finance average service levels without any state assistance. Hawaii and Honolulu counties had revenue shortfalls, that is, revenue raising capacity was insufficient to meet the average level of service to be provided to their respective constituents.

"Winners" after all. The bottom line of all this is that as far as state expenditures are concerned, the neighbor islands have been beneficiaries—"winners," if you will—in the annual pie-slicing contest, receiving more in state grants and services than they have been contributing to the State. Honoluluans have been good neighbors, paying far more in taxes than they are receiving back in grants and services.

The ACIR analysis suggests that Maui and Kauai could do better in raising the money they need, while Hawaii county probably will continue to need an extra portion of the state pie.

Keep in mind, however, that this analysis is relative. As a group, the counties have a practical problem trying to raise user fees and property taxes when their constituents already are paying unusually high taxes to the State. People swamped by high total taxes are in no mood to pay more taxes to the counties simply because those counties may be underfinanced.

Are neighbor islands getting their "fair share" of services and grants from the State? Yes, that and more. Why are all the counties underfinanced as compared to the State? That's another question. Read on.

Getting a fair shake

Neighbor island counties are getting a fair share of state grants. While the City and County of Honolulu gets the most money, on a per person basis the grants to the other counties are much greater.

Honolulu gets the most money of all the counties

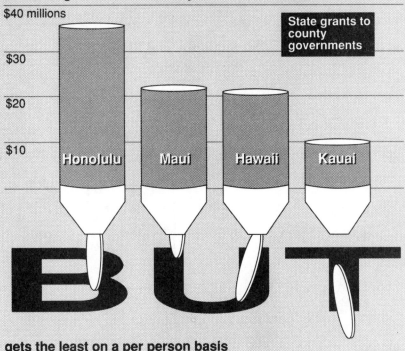

State grants to county governments

gets the least on a per person basis

Per person state grants to county governments

Source: State of Hawaii, Department of Business, Economic Development and Tourism, *Data Book 1991*, table 274.

"I DUNNO ABOUT THIS ROOM TAX TRANSFER—I KINDA LIKE HOW THE COUNTIES GET FUNDING NOW..."

CHAPTER 6

PATERNALISTIC GOVERNMENT

LOWELL L. KALAPA
President
Tax Foundation of Hawaii

"Why is it that the State seems to 'bully' the counties?"

Unlike its counterparts on the Mainland, Hawaii is dominated by a paternalistic, highly centralized state government that taxes residents heavily to provide services traditionally considered the province of local (i.e., county) governments. In principle, governmental decision-making and the financing and delivery of public services should be decentralized to the greatest extent possible. In Hawaii, these functions are almost unbelievably centralized. To understand how we residents of Hawaii could allow this, one must consider the past.

A powerful centralized government is part of the historic fabric of Hawaii. Captain Cook saw it when he landed in 1778, and it was perpetuated with the subsequent establishment of the Hawaiian kingdom and in the flourishing sugar plantations. This centralized rule spilled over into the structure of a territorial government that had the power to set policy throughout the islands. Local government was, at most, a mere afterthought.

Treated like children. From the start, the four counties were treated like children and given limited responsibilities. They were charged with providing only sewer and water services, police and fire protection, and street lighting. Everything else came from "the boss," the territorial government.

And how did the counties pay for the few services they provided? As it does today, the property tax provided the bulk of the counties' revenues. The counties, however, had little control over property taxes. In fact, the counties did not even set their own property-tax rates until 1989.

The counties used to follow a convoluted process which required them to submit their annual budgets to the territorial treasurer showing estimated expenditures, nonproperty tax revenues and the amount remaining to be financed out of the property tax. For Hawaii and Kauai counties, the treasurer then evaluated the need for property taxes and computed the rate. Honolulu and Maui county boards of supervisors were allowed to set the rates but, in all cases, the amount of property taxes raised by each county was set by the territorial legislature. And what if the counties wanted to raise more? Forget it—there was no way it could be done.

Strong federal control through an appointed governor taking orders from Washington, D.C. perpetuated the concept that a strong central government should decide how public services should be paid for and delivered throughout Hawaii.

Constitutional conventions convened both before and after statehood persisted in retaining all taxing power at the territorial/state level, relegating few responsibilities to local or county government. Odd arrangements developed. For example, local government was empowered to hand out traffic citations but resulting revenues went to the territorial/state government. This unusual situation continues today.

In almost every other area, the territorial/state government retained as much power to set policy as it could. Even where functions had been delegated to the counties, the territorial/state government sometimes chose to take them back.

Centralized control. Other evidence of this dictatorship—oops, I mean strong centralized control—occurred immediately after statehood when the equal pay for equal work principle was established in the civil service system. This did not refer to equal pay between the sexes. Rather, it addressed the requirement that all governments pay uniform salaries to employees performing similar jobs, regardless of the level of government or, for that matter, government's ability to pay such salaries.

The unfairness of that requirement was perpetuated with the adoption of collective bargaining early in the 1970s. Since bargaining units represent public workers at both the state and county levels, the outcomes of negotiations and arbitrations are subject to approval by the State and the counties. However, the law gives the State five votes, while the four counties have one vote each. It doesn't take a math whiz to figure out that the State will always control the outcome. This perpetuates the frustration of counties that must pay the same wages as the State, while lacking the revenue resources.

For many years, the counties received a nearly 40 percent share of total collections of the general excise tax. But the State unilaterally replaced this in 1965 with a new system of grants-in-aid. The formula dictated that the size of the grants would be based on each county's "relative fiscal capacity and relative fiscal need." In other words, by some arbitrary analysis as to whether a county was pushing the property tax to the hilt. Of course, politics played a dominant role.

At the same time, a new system of capital improvement allocation was adopted which required state and county cost-sharing. Projects which the State might consider discretionary were put on this track. On the other hand, if the State decided a project was of high priority, a county contribution often was not required. Thus, the State controlled where and when development was to proceed.

As the initial post-statehood boom began to taper in the early 1970s and the State became hard-pressed for revenues, another look was taken at the system of grants-in-aid. The impetus for change came with the federal revenue-sharing program. The federal government did not want the State to use local sharing of federal revenue as an excuse to reduce state assistance to local governments. Therefore, the feds dictated that, if the states wanted revenue-sharing funds, they had to promise not to take away any existing state funds for local governments.

The State of Hawaii was constrained a bit by this, but did its best anyhow to retain control. It refused for the next 15 years to increase annual grants to the counties.

In the meantime, among the hottest topics of debate in the fiscal area at the 1978 constitutional convention were state-county relationships. In the end, the constitutional convention decided that control of the real-property tax system should be turned over to the counties.

Thinly veiled distrust. Students of good government saw this as a small step, but at least it was in the right direction. Still, key political leaders had doubts. As a result, the constitutional convention inserted a provision that effectively postponed a transfer of complete control to the counties for 11 years. This period was one year longer than the date for another constitutional convention—evidence of thinly veiled distrust of the counties. Obviously, the state folks planned to revisit the issue before effective control shifted.

But the people of Hawaii seem to have had an even greater distrust of constitutional conventions. When the question was placed on the ballot in 1986, voters soundly defeated the calling of another convention.

Upon taking control of the property tax, the counties realized that this was not a complete solution to their problems. There was and is a growing mismatch between the property tax (and other available county resources), on the one hand, and their growing responsibilities, on the other. In theory, property taxes are "underutilized" by the counties, and can (and should) be raised. The reality, however, is that residents feel so burdened by their total state and county tax bill that they will not stand for substantial increases in their property taxes.

What had been relatively inexpensive functions of county government 25 years ago have now become very costly due to new federal mandates. The counties have resorted to unfair (and unwise) property-tax rate differentials—taxing nonresidential property at rates up to three times higher than residential rates—and substantial increases to regressive user fees and charges in an attempt to make ends meet.

Time and time again (for example, with respect to mass transit on Oahu), the State has been unwilling to share its tremendous wealth with the counties, insisting instead that the counties raise taxes on their own.

Dominant role. The State's dominant role doesn't apply just to public finances, but to all phases of government policymaking responsibilities. For example, land use policies are controlled, if not dictated, by the State Land Use Commission. Only after this august body has passed judgment on which lands will be reclassified from conservation or agricultural into some higher use do the counties have a say, and then only to the extent of how these lands are to be developed.

A recent sore which continues to fester is how the State has by-passed the counties' authority to oversee construction standards. When the State's affordable-housing super-agency was established in 1988, it was made omnipotent for five years during which it could supersede all other laws governing the use, zoning, planning and development of affordable housing. This in effect allowed the agency to ignore local ordinances governing urban zoning, building codes and construction standards. To say the least, this did not sit well with county officials.

From kingdom to territory to statehood, the people of Hawaii have opted for (or been saddled with) a strong central government despite the fact that local government is closer and more responsive to the people. Does the State bully the counties? Now that you know the history, what do you think?

CHAPTER 7

GOVERNMENT SIZE

JACK P. SUYDERHOUD
Professor of Decision Sciences
College of Business Administration
University of Hawaii

"Has government in Hawaii grown too big?"

A constant concern among taxpayers (here and elsewhere) is that government has grown too big. This is not new. As early as 1880, the German economist Adolph Wagner advanced his "law of rising expenditures" which anticipated that, as societies developed, the demand for government intervention and services would grow. A corollary—call it the "law of money to burn"—says this tendency will be magnified when a tax system regularly generates "excess" revenue.

Hawaii is a relatively high-tax state, where state and local governments collect nearly 30 percent more taxes per person than the national average.

This was not always the case. In the early 1950s, our territory was only slightly above the national average. But for the first 20 years after statehood, tax revenues grew much faster than personal income. By 1975, state and local tax collections were considerably above the national average. Although they declined a bit in the early to mid-1980s, Hawaii today is well above the national average in tax collections.

Different in California. In contrast, California experienced a fiscal revolution in the late 1970s. Its most famous manifestation,

Proposition 13, enacted in 1978, rolled back property taxes. Like Hawaii, California taxes were well above the national average. Thereafter they dropped rapidly to about the national average. Clearly, California demonstrates that if voters want to rebel against high taxes, they can do so.

One reason Hawaii's taxes are high is our relatively low reliance on nontax revenues such as user charges for water, sewer, boat slips, golf course fees, bus fares and university tuition. California has become more reliant on this type of revenue in order to make up for the tax shortfalls caused by Proposition 13 and other tax revolt measures.

Not surprisingly, expenditure trends in Hawaii are similar to the revenue patterns. After all, governments do not collect money to have it sit around; they generally spend it as fast as possible. Hawaii has always been a relatively big-spender. In territorial days, this was made possible by federal grants. Between statehood and the mid-1970s, government spending boomed in Hawaii. It dwarfed even the robust growths of the national and California averages. Since then, however, spending growth has slowed.

California again provides a contrast to this experience. Its state-local spending also grew substantially and was above the national average. The tax revolt of the late 1970s, however, forced spending down to the national average.

California enjoyed remarkable growth and prosperity until the early 1990s when a severe national recession whacked it particularly hard. That state's fiscal crisis in 1992 was not the result of its tax revolt some 15 years earlier. Even so, if Hawaii ever decides to roll back the size of its government, there are much better ways to do it than those used in California.

State employment booms. The largest component of any government's budget is for wages and salaries. Since before statehood, Hawaii has been above the national average in the number of government workers per 10,000 population. Up to 1977, that figure grew much more rapidly than the population, to about 540 government workers per 10,000 population. That was 12.5 percent above the national average of 480. This relationship has changed little since then. Reflecting the effects of its tax revolt, California started out with higher-than-average government employment, but is now below the national average.

Government payroll, as a percent of state personal income, grew considerably between the 1950s and the late 1970s. Hawaii government payrolls were 6.6 percent of personal income in 1957 compared to the national average of 5.6 percent. Currently, it is 8.4 percent and the national average is 8.3 percent.

In spite of the higher cost of living, Hawaii government payrolls in the 1980s were consistent with the national average. Since Hawaii had more workers than the national average, these workers must have been paid less than the national average. There may be good reasons for this. For example, the fringe benefits of government employment here are higher than elsewhere. In addition, and in contrast to many other states where "low-skill" jobs such as refuse collection are privatized, Hawaii has many "low-skill" public-sector employees. On the other hand, it may be as my boss says, "We make up for the high cost of living by paying you less."

For the two decades starting in the mid-1950s, state governments in general experienced high rates of growth. This was largely due to the higher voter demands that governments provide goods and services ranging from infrastructure to education. During this period, states enacted new sales and income taxes to finance their new expenditure responsibilities. For Hawaii, the experience was similar, except the growth rates were higher. This was due in part to the stronger underlying population and economic growth of Hawaii. The infrastructure requirements for this were greater than for most other states.

Why Hawaii's government keeps growing. The 1980s saw a reversal of this trend in most states. Nationally, state and local governments stopped their relative growth. In many states—California, for example—state and local governments actually shrank. This was not the case in Hawaii for several reasons.

First, Hawaii has long been a "centralized" state. This has resulted in an inflexible bureaucratic government, public sector unions with considerable power, and an overall lack of innovation and efficiencies.

Second, for better of worse, Hawaii has a long tradition of paternalistic "rulers." Where other states have "privatized" public services, Hawaii has done the opposite. For example, after-school child care was provided by the private sector until 1991 when the state-financed "A+"

program put them out of business. Increasingly, the State and counties are providing housing, a traditionally private-sector enterprise. On Oahu, traffic reports once were provided by private-sector radio stations at no expense to taxpayers; now the State Department of Transportation pays for it. When something is not quite what the people want, the tradition in Hawaii is to ask government to step in.

Third, the underlying economy was strong prior to 1992. Economic growth results in a demand for an expansion of public services. Also, economic growth provides exceptional tax-revenue growth. Hawaii relies on a broad-based general excise tax and a progressive income tax, both of which are exceptionally responsive to economic growth. For every 10 percent growth of personal income, state tax collections are estimated to increase by almost 12 percent. Our political leaders have these "money trees" at their disposal.

Fourth, the fact that we have a one-party state has reduced the likelihood that anyone will "shake up the system." Accountability is reduced and tough questions either do not get asked or, if raised, are ignored. The lack of general public input into annual fiscal decisions may have a role here.

So, has government in Hawaii become too big? The answer depends on how you feel about what government has done and how well it has done it. My feeling is that it *has* become too big. It is not responsive, creative or flexible. It is not using our tax dollars efficiently; it should be able to do more with less. In Hawaii, the combination of a tax structure that causes revenues to grow faster than the economy, a centralized government with an entrenched bureaucracy, people with a tradition of overdependence on government, and a one-party power structure pretty much insures that an already-big government will continue to get bigger.

STAR-BULLETIN *CORKY* '87

High-tax state

As a percent of state personal income, state-local government revenues grew between the mid-1950s and mid-1970s. But unlike California, which experienced a fiscal revolution in the late 1970s, Hawaii remains a high-tax state.

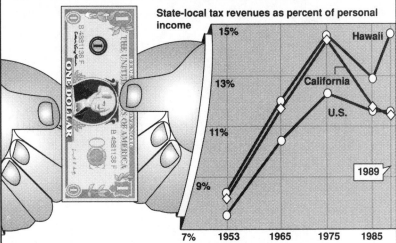

State-local tax revenues as percent of personal income

Hawaii
California
U.S.
1989

15%
13%
11%
9%
7%

1953   1965   1975   1985

Source: Advisory Commission on Intergovernmental Relations, *Significant Features of Fiscal Federalism, 1991, Vol. II; Revenues and Expenditures,* M-176-II, Washington, D.C., October 1991, p. 180.

"IN THE LEGISLATURE, YOU MAY CHARGE OVERTIME TO FINISH A JOB YOU FAIL TO DO WITHIN YOUR REGULAR HOURS, KEOKI ... HERE, YOU'RE JUST FIRED."

CHAPTER 8

GOVERNMENT EFFICIENCY

GEORGE MASON
Editorial Page Editor and Publisher Emeritus
Pacific Business News

"What's wrong with letting government in Hawaii get bigger each year?"

"Efficiency" is interpreted in opposite ways by the public and private sectors. A business is efficient or it goes broke. The more efficient it is, the more money the owners and employees realize. There is motivation for efficiency.

In government, promotions seldom are based on productivity. Other factors prevail, such as keeping an agency out of trouble ("covering up" effectively) or being well-liked or not rocking anyone's boat.

Further, most promotions and pay raises depend on how many people you supervise. Picture this: an entry-level typist can deliberately let the work pile up while appearing busy. When the work isn't getting out on time, the bureaucratic assumption is that the workload exceeds the capacity of the typist to handle it and therefore more help is needed. Going from Typist I (entry level) to Typist II, and supervising the new entry-level Typist I, means a pay raise.

A classic example. I was personally involved in a classic example of this kind of thinking in the late 1950s when I was the State Director of Economic Development. I needed an experienced research analyst. The personnel people said I could have one only if that person were to supervise a less-experienced one—which I neither wanted nor needed. After a six-month battle (even trying to get the governor to intervene), I gave up and hired two research analysts in order to get one with experience. My department went from 10 to 12 employees.

That was one more employee than I needed, but still a pretty small staff. How could I run a cabinet-level department with multiple functions with so few people? Simple. I contracted out much of the work and didn't have to contend with a permanent staff which would require ongoing make-work projects to justify its existence. At that time the State Department of Planning and Research (which also contracted for a good deal of its work) had 22 employees. When Governor John Burns took over, he merged the two departments, creating one agency with a total of 34 people. Within less than a year it was up to 100, and before long it topped 200.

At the end of 1962, some 17,000 were on the state payroll. At the end of 1991, there were over 62,000—a rate of increase far beyond that of Hawaii's population. Is state government more efficient now than it was 30 years ago? No. And it wasn't any too efficient then.

Lavish spending. During the 1992 session of the legislature, a big fuss was made over the fact that most legislators had been traveling first-class. A few vigilant souls also complained about the $700 chairs that legislators had bought for themselves.

The state bureaucracy is rife with nonessential spending. Some agencies have much higher-priced furniture in first-class private office buildings all over Honolulu. A couple of thousand park for peanuts in garages especially built for them or in private downtown spaces that charge others $200 or more a month. While 76 legislators may be living high with our money, thousands of people we can't vote out of office are emptying our pockets at a rate most taxpayers wouldn't believe.

While Hawaii is far from being alone in government inefficiency, our problem is worse than many realize. Perhaps this reflects an ethnic tendency that was used to keep people in line when sugar and pineapple were dominant. There was no open questioning of authority, and authority figures were given deity status. That attitude, only slightly modified, still prevails.

No government is efficient. The reason no government is efficient is because there is no risk, no bottom line, no effective way to light a fire under workers who see no connection between their employer's success and their own job security. How do you motivate a protected bureaucracy?

A classic case of lack of results when the voters do get good and mad is what happened in the aftermath of Proposition 13 (spending and taxing limitation) in California. Public services deteriorated, seriously affecting taxpayers. All the while the bureaucracy moaned in excruciating pain about how overworked and understaffed it was.

Have you ever heard any government worker from department head on down say the current level of staffing was adequate? Of course not. Bureaucrats always need more people. Not to get the job done, but to justify more pay for supervising more underlings.

Always bigger. Government is always bigger than it ought to be. Among the reasons are: (1) to stay long in office, politicians must make promises to constituents and special interests on which they must at least do a good job of pretending to deliver; (2) the rising influence of public employee unions has given government workers more job protection than they already had; (3) career bureaucrats have an uncanny knack for expanding their workload and thus their pay checks and titles; and, finally, (4) the electorate is distressingly indifferent, as reflected by the fact that fewer than half the people eligible to vote actually go to the polls.

Can anything be done to change this situation, to reduce the bureaucracy and thus its burden on taxpayers? Part of the answer is in what is commonly called privatization.

All of government, naturally, can't be privatized. But many jurisdictions have realized considerable savings in activities customarily handled by civil servants. I'm certain that honest private-management deals (no cumshaw) would vastly improve many public services and facilities.

There is always a danger of shenanigans such as noncompetitive contracts, "acceptable" cost overruns, incompetent vendors and even graft on the part of public officials. But if there are enough citizen watchdogs such as Common Cause, the League of Women Voters and inquiring news media, this could be kept in check. I am confident that, in the long run, privatization would save a great deal of money and get work done more quickly.

The problem is not in the civil service *per se*, which came about because public employment in the old days amounted to public plunder by ward heelers. Rather, government is inherently inefficient. Thus, the best solution would be to minimize the number of civil servants and to hire the private sector to perform as much of government's work as possible.

I'd like to see the State of Hawaii contract out the deposit of tax revenue in interest-bearing accounts on the date of receipt, not three weeks later. And I'd like to see each agency contract out the collection of money owed to it. Some parking fines have been outstanding for years. Then there is the payment of money owed to private businesses. In fiscal 1991, state agencies paid half a million dollars in interest on past-due bills. If a private business can pay its bills on time, why can't a government which may have more than a billion dollars lying around at any given time?

Time for action. It is time for some serious moves toward privatization. We are not going to eliminate the bureaucracy entirely, but it can be effectively reduced. In return, public expenditures and the drain on taxpayers can be sharply reduced. The government employee unions will resist, but taxpayers are losing their cool over excessive taxes and too much government in their lives.

What will it take to set these changes in motion? Some brave politician in a position to make it happen is likely to come along in this decade. The people will approve even if the unions don't.

Scales of justice

CHAPTER 9

ROLE OF GOVERNMENT

CHRISTOPHER GRANDY
Visiting Assistant Professor of Economics
University of Hawaii

L. DEW KANESHIRO
Gender and Other Fairness Project Coordinator
Hawaii State Judiciary

"When is government intervention in the economy warranted?"

This book deals with important and perplexing issues facing the people of Hawaii. From land use regulation to public education to environmental protection, it questions government's role in society. Some chapters, written by economists, are critical of one or more aspects of government intervention. This may lead you to think economists see *no* role for government in the economy. That would be a mistake. Economists actually have a long-standing appreciation of government's role in the affairs of civilized society. Indeed, economic thinking provides some helpful guidelines for that role.

Most economists expect government to address problems that arise when private market transactions fail for one reason or another. To understand the ways government can best do this, you must first understand why many people place great faith in private markets.

The marvels of the market. Much of our daily activity takes place without the direct involvement of government. We purchase gasoline and groceries, work in private businesses, attend movies, and so on. Economists regard these activities as "private" in the sense that the self-interest of the parties usually generates mutually satisfactory results.

Respect for markets comes from two aspects of these private activities. First, each transaction seems to leave both the buyer and seller better off than before. The gas-station owner makes a profitable sale and you have fuel in your car. Presumably, the gas-station owner values the sale more highly than the gas and you value the gas more highly than the money you paid for it (otherwise one of you would not have agreed to the transaction). It's a win-win result. Second, to the extent these transactions take place within a competitive market, they involve prices set by the forces of demand and supply. The price system coordinates your demand for gas with the owner's willingness to supply it.

The combination of these two aspects of private transactions—improved welfare and competitive prices—forms the basis of an important insight of modern economic analysis: perfectly competitive markets efficiently allocate goods and services and thereby improve people's welfare.

This analysis suggests a hypothetical world that would require no government. Competitive markets in all goods and services would exist, and people could acquire those goods and services at the lowest cost. Further, no other way of allocating the goods and services among society's members could improve the welfare of some without reducing the well-being of others. This hypothetical world provides a benchmark against which to compare the real world and helps identify situations in which government involvement may improve social well-being.

Inefficient competition. A case for government involvement can be made by recognizing limits to the efficiency of competition itself. Imagine, for example, Oahu served by ten electric companies. Their competition for your business would presumably drive rates down to the level of costs. This may sound good from your perspective as consumer, but ultimately you could pay more for electricity. Like most utilities, electric companies face high fixed costs. Each of the ten companies would invest in costly plant and equipment, establish a network to deliver electricity to households, and hire personnel to handle billing and customer service. Sound like wasteful duplication of effort? Most economists would agree. Indeed, the most efficient organization for industries like electricity may leave room for only one firm. The industry can then spread high fixed costs over a large number of sales, rather than forcing each of many firms to bear such costs separately.

But one firm is the very antithesis of competition! Thus, industries that (for technological reasons) prove more efficient with only one firm provide an exception to the hypothetical competitive model. This, in turn, may call for a governmental mechanism to assure that the firm does not use its monopoly status to raise prices far above costs. That is why Hawaii has a Public Utilities Commission to review requests for rate increases by public utilities like HECO.

Third-party effects. Goods and services whose consumption or production affect people other than the buyer and seller provide another rationale for government involvement. Such transactions are private, but have "third-party effects."

Consider a manufacturing process that generates undesirable wastewater. The cost-minimizing company without government rules and regulations will dispose of the waste as cheaply as possible by dumping into streams and ocean, adversely affecting everyone who uses those resources. The dumping of sludge by the private Hawaii Kai sewage treatment plant in 1988-1989 illustrates how the profit motive can prompt firms to cut corners at the expense of the environment. Government may legitimately prevent these producers from doing what competitive pressures might otherwise force them to do. Because environmental matters are particularly fraught with third-party effects, government must intervene to protect Mother Earth.

Third-party effects can also take a positive form. For example, universal education bestows benefits on both direct recipients and society as a whole. A well-educated population tends to make a productive and wealthy society. If government did not provide free or low-cost schooling, those with few resources would, in most cases, fail to attain their potential, and the larger community would suffer as a result. We may therefore reasonably require all taxpayers to contribute to the costs of public education.

Public goods. A third example of a legitimate government role in

the economy relates to "public goods." These are goods and services for which one person's consumption does not reduce the supply available for others. Private producers may find denying access to nonpaying consumers impractical or even impossible. This makes private market arrangements very difficult.

Consider police services. Suppose you and your neighbors hire a private security firm to patrol the area. The entire neighborhood would become more secure. Yet some of the neighbors might refuse to pay, hoping to get a free ride. If everyone acted this way, no private firm would supply security services, even though people generally value them. The government can resolve this problem by financing such services with tax dollars.

Summary. This discussion does not exhaust the economic arguments in favor of governmental intervention in the economy, but it covers a widely accepted area. As you read the other chapters in this book, keep in mind these economic arguments for government. If a chapter deals primarily with private goods for which a competitive market seems well-suited, then you may understand why that author questions government involvement.

If government appears substantially and actively involved in some area of the economy, can you identify a natural monopoly, third-party effect, or public good issue? There are good reasons for government involvement in the economy and we should expect our political leaders to articulate those reasons in each particular case.

CHAPTER 10

SEWAGE PROBLEMS

JAMES E.T. MONCUR
Professor of Economics
University of Hawaii

"How bad is Honolulu's sewage problem?"

Honolulu Mayor Frank Fasi has said it would cost $1.1 billion to upgrade Oahu's wastewater treatment plants from "primary" to "secondary" treatment, resulting in higher sewage fees by a factor of two and a half. Adding insult to injury, he asserted all this money would produce little benefit.

Lawyers from the Sierra Club Legal Defense Fund (SCLDF) have suggested the cost of secondary treatment probably would be less than a third of the Mayor's estimates, and that Honolulu should conform to the federal requirement for secondary treatment, just like everyone else, regardless of the cost. At the same time, some Kailua residents clamor for "tertiary" treatment of effluent from the plant serving them.

Before we try to make sense out of this, I need to explain "primary," "secondary," and "tertiary" treatment of sewage. **Primary** treatment filters out about 30 percent of suspended solids and removes an equal proportion of oxygen-depleting organic matter. **Secondary** treatment raises these figures to 85 percent, while **tertiary** processing involves nearly complete removal of pollutants as well as disinfection of the effluent. Effluent that has received secondary or tertiary treatment can be used for irrigation or to recharge groundwater aquifers, but all three processes leave residual solids that must be disposed of in some way.

Now that you know the treatment options, you should understand why the choices must be made by government rather than each of us individually. People usually decide how to spend their own money and in the process indicate what has value to them. Some people go first-class. Others with equal (or even greater) funds choose second or even third-class. Decisions as to what and how much to buy are made separately, in a way that will maximize value to each buyer.

Buying wastewater treatment is more complicated. One person's decision on type and level of treatment matters a great deal to that person's neighbors. Buying less and accepting the consequences might be OK to one buyer whose neighbors may object strongly. Buying less may not only invoke revolting aesthetic images, but also affect the health of those neighbors, the cost of their health care and perhaps other costs such as contamination of their drinking water. Because "third-party effects" dominate this area, a private market for sewage treatment would not reflect in full the benefits of that treatment.

Hard choices. Hence government must enter the picture. Fundamental economic questions remain: what to produce, how much to produce, where to produce, how to produce, who will pay and who gets to use it. But government has little information relevant to answering these questions. There is no market to which the government can look in order to gauge the intensity of demand for more or less sewage treatment.

Other things being equal, virtually everyone prefers more environmental quality to less. Some people are especially strong for environmental purity and would be willing to pay first-class fare to get it. Others, for whatever reason, are not so particular. Unfortunately, the technology and institutions for making decisions on sewage, air quality and other environmental factors do not allow each person his or her own preferred level. We're all in this one together.

Pragmatically speaking, some would assert that the Environmental Protection Agency (EPA) has settled the matter for us. EPA standards, for example, call for secondary treatment of all sewage effluent before it's dumped into receiving waters. But most cities pipe their treated sewage into a river or lake. Honolulu has a very large Pacific Ocean to receive its discharge. Because of this, EPA has the power to waive the secondary requirement for Honolulu as long as effluent can be "deep-sixed" without adverse effects.

In the context of the primary/secondary treatment controversy in Honolulu, we should note that nine of the City's 12 sewage treatment plants (not counting private facilities) already had met the secondary standard as of 1992. The two largest, however, did not. The Sand Island and Honouliuli plants together account for some 86 percent of the total flow processed by city plants. As primary treatment facilities, these two remove about 30 percent of solids and oxygen-demanding organic materials. What's left is then piped several thousand feet offshore to the ocean depths. Does this dumping adversely affect the ocean?

Ocean disposal. The effects of sewage outfalls on the ocean or coastal environment have been studied extensively. University of Hawaii scientist Richard Grigg was personally involved in many of these studies. He has concluded and publicly stated that "secondary treatment for Oahu's existing outfalls offers no advantages over primary treatment in terms of environmental impact on coral reefs, reef fishes or plankton communities." Pollutants are widely and quickly dispersed by ocean currents which take effluent away from the shore and thus out of harm's way. Viral components die off within minutes, posing no threat. Numerous studies agree that the sewage effluent causes no appreciable negative impact to the ocean environment. In fact, some scientists believe secondary treatment may be environmentally *worse* than primary treatment.

Environmentalists remain unconvinced. Their experts claim city studies have ignored certain marine life forms, like coral or crab zooplankton or larval fish, and have simply assumed ocean currents will keep effluent away from shore. Similarly, Kailua residents, noticing occasional algal blooms in Kailua Bay and pollution in Kaelepulu Stream, ascribe these problems to discharge from the Kailua treatment plant (a secondary treatment facility) and insist that the plant be expanded and upgraded to the tertiary level.

To an extent, these questions of fact can be answered by further research. The University of Hawaii Water Resources Research Center, for example, did extensive studies of Kailua Bay in early 1992 and concluded that pollutants in the bay come not from the sewage treatment plant, but from natural animal and plant life in the marshes and streams feeding into the bay. The ocean outfall, moreover, feeds

73

into currents moving northerly, away from Kailua Beach.

Closed beaches. Occasional bypasses at treatment plants have sent untreated sewage directly into popular ocean recreation areas and have contributed to the impression that the plants are inadequate. The causes of bypasses, however, generally have been power failures, maintenance activities and faulty sewage mains. None of these problems would be eliminated by an upgrade from secondary to tertiary treatment. Furthermore, old sewer lines have developed extensive leaks, allowing storm water runoff flowing into the sewer system during heavy rainfall to overwhelm the treatment plant. Why not fix these problems first, and *then* decide what, if anything, to do with the plant? The pipes need fixing, and the other problems need solving, in any event.

Other questions are less amenable to scientific inquiry and will probably continue to vex policy makers. For example, the qualifier in phrases like "no appreciable negative impacts" means different things to people with different attitudes about nature. Some might be content to dump *untreated* sewage into the ocean, as long as profits stay high and the effluent lands on somebody else's beach. On the other end of the spectrum, ardent environmentalists might be quite willing to contribute their share of the enormous cost required to attain their high standards—and to insist, through judicial and legislative processes, that the rest of the population do likewise.

Balancing costs and benefits. Uneven distribution of benefits or costs can induce different strategic behaviors. Suppose I, a (hypothetical) resident of Kailua, consider tertiary treatment of sewage to be worth, say, $40 a month. But such treatment would cost each beneficiary $60 a month. To me, it would not be worth the cost.

However, suppose government contributes part of the costs, say the equivalent of $25 a month per beneficiary. My personal share of the costs will then be $35 plus my share of the extra taxes needed to raise the government's $25. Since my share of the taxes (which would be paid by many taxpayers, rather than the relatively few residents of Kailua) will be small, the investment in tertiary treatment suddenly looks good again. I get something worth $40 to me, and my direct cost is only $35.

Beneficiaries in this scenario would be indulging in a game developed by decades of practice in federal water, transportation and other projects and sharpened, until the 1980s, with federal subsidies to sewage treatment plants. Government must ask: are the benefits of tertiary treatment (as opposed to secondary treatment) worth the full costs? Or are the beneficiaries counting on achieving something for which they would not willingly pay, if they had to cover the full cost by themselves? Unfortunately, these kinds of questions do not have clear-cut answers.

Another type of strategic behavior may be significant here. As a means of enforcing EPA regulations, groups and individuals have legal standing to bring suit over perceived violations of the regulations. The SCLDF has been particularly active in this area. Fund lawyers probably share their clients' relatively high evaluation of environmental benefits. Their long-term career paths, moreover, depend to some extent on their success in finding such perceived violations and bringing suit successfully—regardless of the overall benefits and costs of the regulation in a particular setting. Hence the incentive of the SCLDF to sue the city to get secondary treatment at Honouliuli and Sand Island, even in the face of evidence that primary-treated waste has no appreciable negative effect on the ocean environment.

Early discussion of environmental problems often urged total elimination of pollution. But as long as humans, other animals and plants continue to enjoy the processes of life, we will produce undesirable side effects. To ameliorate these effects requires consumption of scarce resources. Hence we must decide, given the costs, how much pollution we can live with, including what level and degree of sewage treatment we wish to provide for ourselves.

There is, in principle, a socially optimal level of sewage treatment. Unfortunately, no one knows what it is or has a really good idea how to determine it. EPA regulations result from political processes and give little consideration to balancing benefits and costs.

It makes no sense for Honolulu to be subject to the standards applied to most inland cities. There is a big difference between dumping sewage in the ocean and dumping it in a lake or river. At least that's what the scientists tell us.

CHAPTER 11

GOVERNMENT SPENDING: SMOKE & MIRRORS

PAUL H. BREWBAKER
Economist
Bank of Hawaii

LOWELL L. KALAPA
President
Tax Foundation of Hawaii

RANDALL W. ROTH
Professor of Law
William S. Richardson
School of Law
University of Hawaii

MARCIA Y. SAKAI
Assistant Professor
Business Administration
and Economics Division
University of Hawaii at Hilo

"How much does our state government spend each year?"

You have asked a simple question and you probably expect a simple answer. Instead, we will tell you about the Hawaii State Legislature's increasing use of practices that obscure the level of state spending and thereby make it impossible to give you a simple answer.

We begin by emphasizing the importance of a straightforward budget process. It allows bureaucrats to keep track of government finances and helps politicians understand what they can and cannot afford. Equally important, it promotes accountability by providing voters with the basic information to evaluate the job being done by their political leaders. Practices that make it difficult to understand the budget process should be followed only when there is a good reason.

The practices that we are about to detail obscure the budget process without providing a benefit. Because of them, voters are likely to think (1) the level of state spending is lower than it really is, (2) there is no surplus at a time when that may not be true, and (3) taxation has been no higher than necessary to fund current policy initiatives.

Special (and revolving) funds. Most government receipts go into what's called the general fund. This supports schools, health care and sanitation, public safety, welfare and other day-to-day operations of government. But a growing amount gets put into separate accounts, referred to as special and revolving funds.

The size of the general fund is important. The two most important reasons for our purposes relate to provisions of the Hawaii State Constitution. The first places a "spending ceiling" on the amount of general funds that can be appropriated in any year. The second sometimes mandates a rebate when there is a substantial surplus of general funds. We'll tell you more about these constitutional provisions later.

Special funds usually are financed by revenues from a specific source and earmarked for a specific purpose. One example is the highway special fund financed by fuel taxes, vehicle-weight taxes, and registration fees, and used only to build and maintain roads. Another example is the airports special fund obtained from landing fees, concessionaire lease payments and aviation fuel taxes, and used only for airport-related needs. Revolving funds are similar to special funds, but typically are established with an initial lump-sum allocation or with a series of installments. These amounts are then made available to particular programs which are expected to replenish the fund. An example is the $120 million loan that provided a kick-start to the State's affordable housing program. To keep our explanation reasonably simple, we will treat revolving funds as a type of special fund (since the effect for our purposes is the same).

Special-fund balances do not revert to the general fund each fiscal year but are carried forward to be used in future years. Because special funds traditionally involve activities that generate their own revenue, they are left on their own to operate with less frequent legislative review.

The usual reasons for using special funds are to target a tax so that a specific project (such as road repairs) is paid for by the direct beneficiaries (such as users of the repaired roads) and to insulate certain basic functions from economic or political influences.

The spending ceiling. In an attempt to keep government expenditures in line with taxpayers' ability to pay taxes, the Hawaii State Constitution puts a limit on increases in expenditures from the general fund. The "ceiling" is based on a fixed formula. There is, however, considerable flexibility. The legislature can exceed the spending ceiling by putting a public spotlight on this phase of the budget process and approving any such action by a two-thirds vote, rather than the usual majority. That's the proper mechanism for exceeding the ceiling.

The loophole. The legislature, to avoid this public spotlight and tougher voting requirement, has exploited a loophole. By simply reclassifying an arbitrary amount of general funds to special-fund status, the level of general-fund appropriations drops "magically" (as professional illusionists like to say), typically to an amount comfortably below the constitutionally mandated spending ceiling. Has spending been reduced? Of course not. Has the spending ceiling been exceeded? Technically no. Do smoke and mirrors hide reality from the taxpayers?

Before answering this last question, we will share a quote from the Hawaii State Tax Review Commission. Using the gentle language one expects from an eclectic, nonpartisan body, the commission put it this way: "Special funds that merely set aside general fund revenues for general fund expenditures cannot be justified; they restrict budget flexibility, create inefficiencies, and lessen accountability. The purpose for such funds may be laudable and worthwhile, but the use of this type of special fund is not. Desired programs and services can be given priority under the normal budget process without resorting to this type of financing." This is a nice way of telling legislators that their hand has been caught in the cookie jar. If they want more cookies they should ask for them properly.

The commission's concerns led to a visit by the legislative auditor. Among other things, this government watchdog recommended that the 1992 legislature stop using 22 of the many special and revolving funds then in use. Unfortunately, the recommendations were deferred, just as they had been the year before.

Another consequence of reclassifying general funds is that only general funds are counted in applying the mandatory rebate provision. By pumping money into special funds, the legislature avoids being forced to rebate taxes to taxpayers.

Lawmakers are understandably reluctant to give back money that was politically difficult to raise. Tucking that money away in a special fund increases the chances that their constituents won't expect its return or demand that it be used in a particular way. In this fashion, the legislature during the late 1980's and early 1990's was able to create the illusion that taxes were producing just enough revenue to run the state, rather than generating a surplus.

Another questionable practice. The legislature uses another back-alley to avoid the public spotlight—going over the constitutional spending ceiling without declaring how much in aggregate the ceiling is being exceeded. This occurs because additional, and by themselves small, spending bills come to the floor for approval *after* the legislature has voted to exceed the spending ceiling. This follows the letter but not the spirit of the constitution. Once totaled, the many "small" appropriations during the 1989-1991 fiscal biennium exceeded the spending ceiling by $500 million! That doesn't take into account the even larger amount that was diverted into special and revolving funds!

Are we advocating a tax cut? Not necessarily. We're mostly interested in open and honest accounting. If our elected representatives want to exceed the constitutional spending ceiling properly (under a public spotlight and by a two-thirds vote) and within the spirit of that provision (by making clear the extent to which the ceiling is being exceeded), they can do so. In some situations, it may be highly desirable that they go through the ceiling. But it should not be done in ways calculated to mislead.

Special funds have become a New Age pork barrel for a variety of otherwise laudable initiatives that for some reason can't seem to stand normal budget scrutiny. Some are one-shot deals, designed to hide fat as an alternative to tax-rebate liposuction. Others commit the State to general fund revenue diversions lasting five, seven or even ten years.

General funds diverted into special funds during good times are generally not returned during the bad. The wrong programs get cut first when money is tight. Basic public services are likely to suffer most.

And there is the problem of raised expectations. People quickly grow to rely on the public services made possible by special funds and excess spending. What will happen when revenues fall or don't keep up with spending demands? Perhaps the "piggy bank" of special funds can be tapped. But if that money runs out, will the illusion vanish into a call for tax increases to avoid the pain of eliminating services?

Primary issue is honesty. According to many in the legislature, the spending ceiling "gets in the way." After all, if the money is there (and it certainly was in the late 1980s and early 1990s) why not use available loopholes to fund worthwhile special programs as they come along? The simple answer is that government should be honest with the people it governs.

EDUCATION SECOND TO NONE... HEALTH SERVICES SECOND TO NONE... SOCIAL PROGRAMS SECOND TO NONE...

"AFTER A WHILE, WE GET INURED TO THINGS..."

CHAPTER 12

TAX HELL?

ROBERT EBEL

(Formerly UH Professor of Economics)
Director, State Fiscal Services
Policy Economic Group
KPMG Peat Marwick Main & Co.
Washington, D.C.

"Is Hawaii a 'Tax Hell'?"

Auwe! When they picked up the January 1992 issue of *Money* magazine and saw Hawaii referred to as a "Tax Hell," Alice and Arnie Aloha decided to take action. They packed up the keiki, tutu and popoki, and headed for "Tax Heaven"—Alaska. That's right, from Kaimuki to Kodiak. And why not? According to the magazine (January 1992, page 74), the Aloha family will save a whopping $4,680 on their state and local tax bill.

This silly little vignette is overly dramatic, but it reflects the magazine's unspoken message—it's best to live in a "low-tax" state. In fairness to *Money*, it is not the only one playing the annual "tax-ranking game." Players include other reputable magazines, business and labor associations, and conservative and liberal research groups.

The ranking game is popular because people everywhere want to know if their taxes are "too high." Individual states keep an eye on these lists, too. Why? Because a state whose tax burden is significantly "out of line" will lose businesses to states with lower taxes. Jobs will be lost and total state income and product will decline. In short, everyone in that state will be adversely affected by its ranking. Consequently, it seems only logical to determine the likelihood of this by reference to tax levels in other states.

Simple measures. Two of the most common measures of tax level are ratios of taxes collected to population (per-capita tax burdens), and tax burden per $1,000 of household income. *Money*'s index is a mix, calculating the taxes paid currently by a "typical" subscriber family of four.

These simple measures provide easily calculated, quick, and consistent comparisons but these merits are also the source of inherent shortcomings. Consequently, when comparing state rankings, five caveats should be considered.

First, the rankings assume that state and local economies are closed, without movement of goods and services, factors of production, and even consumers, across borders. Accordingly, the numbers fail to take into account that tax costs may be shifted to nonresidents. For example, the fact that roughly a third of Hawaii's excise tax is borne by nonresidents is not reflected in its tax collections numerator.

Second, the ratios give no hint that services are related to tax levels. Residents of low-tax states often (but not always!) receive fewer services than do residents of high-tax states. Nor do these ratios indicate whether a state has legitimately greater spending "needs" (for example, more children of school age or families requiring social assistance) than others.

Third, the "fairness" of distribution of taxes is not considered in these measures. Nor do they address the issue of who benefits from government spending.

Fourth, tax collections, population and income are assumed to be unrelated. Thus, the ratios ignore the possibility that higher taxes and government expenditures may result in better services that attract new businesses and ultimately lead to higher personal income. In other words, an extra dollar in state taxes can result in an extra dime of income for the taxpayers. Of course, this process can also work the other way— higher state taxes can discourage job growth and result in less income for the taxpayer in future years. The point is that not all expenditures have the same effect.

Fifth, the numbers do not account for the fact that the prices of such inputs to produce public services as wages, gasoline prices and the cost of asphalt will differ among states.

Guidelines. All of this suggests some guidelines. First, ask the simple question: might the group issuing the numbers have a hidden agenda such as reducing certain taxes or raising (or at least not lowering) taxes in order to promote some special-interest spending.

Second, recognize that, even if there is no special bias, the numbers just don't tell the whole story. It's up to you (and your elected representatives) to piece together a lot more information before concluding that taxes in Hawaii are "too high" or "too low."

Third, avoid loaded terms like "Tax Hell" and "Tax Heaven." The issue is too important for pejorative rhetoric.

Following these guidelines will require considerable effort, but it is not a hopeless task. Once all the caveats have been noted, policymakers and citizens alike must use their best collective judgment in addressing the issue of whether Hawaii's taxes are "too high." This is one of the reasons for the constitutional requirement that a tax review commission be formed every five years to look at things like the adequacy, efficiency and fairness of Hawaii's tax system.

Hawaii was once at the very bottom of *Money's* list—their "Tax Hell." But at that time property taxes were ignored (property taxes are quite low in Hawaii, in comparison to other states). Now that they are taken into account (along with income taxes, sales taxes and death taxes), Hawaii has risen to number 35 on *Money's* 1992 list. This adjustment in methodology was an improvement, and *Money* has contributed much by bringing the matter of relative state tax burden to the public's attention. Whether taxes in Hawaii are "too high," however, requires more than a review of *Money's* (or any other player's) ranking game score card. The following chapter is a good next step.

CHAPTER 13

LEVEL OF TAXES

PAUL H. BREWBAKER
Economist
Bank of Hawaii

"Are taxes in Hawaii too high?"

The answer is—drum roll, please—an unequivocal "it depends." Not satisfied? OK, here's what we're up against as we try to find a more definitive answer.

For one thing, it depends on whether you think the level of public services provided by state and county governments in Hawaii is too high, too low, or just about right. Oh sure, there's fat that could be cut, but that's the nature of the beast. Efficient government is an oxymoron. That's not to say some efficiency gains cannot be achieved but, even in this best of all possible worlds, these gains probably would be a one-shot deal. It might be more constructive to debate the level of government services. You tell me, is the current level of public services too high?

Do you think the distribution of responsibilities for the provision of public services between state and county governments is correct or incorrect? Hawaii's system of government and revenue collection is centralized at the state level. State expenditures in 1989 comprised 77 percent of all state and local government expenditures in Hawaii, compared to a national average of only 59 percent. Only one state (Delaware) had a higher percentage at that time. Hawaii's relatively high percentage reflects the consolidation at the state level of functions usually provided by counties or school districts on the Mainland. Such a concentration leads to higher, "urban" standards statewide. A shift of responsibilities to the counties arguably would lower tax burdens on the neighbor islands compared to Oahu because salaries of affected government workers living on neighbor islands would be lower.

Question of fairness. It also depends on whether, taking the level of public services as given, you think the tax burden is unfairly borne by residents versus nonresidents. In some states, this might not seem like an important issue, but interstate and international trade comprise more than two-thirds of Hawaii's gross product. This means that nonresidents are wound inextricably into the economic fabric of Hawaii and the forms of tax revenue generated by its economy.

One point cannot be minimized: the constant presence of large numbers of tourists consuming many public services significantly complicates measuring the tax burden. On an average day, more tourists are in Hawaii than residents of any of the neighbor-island counties—more, in fact, than the resident populations of Maui and Kauai counties combined. Two out of every five persons on Maui on any given day are tourists. One out of every four on Kauai is a tourist. Imagine a situation in which 15 percent of the adult population were randomly exempted from state income taxes. You have roughly that situation in Hawaii. That many adults pay taxes only on their retail purchases or through the property and room taxes paid by their hotels.

Despite these and other complications, some objective measures of relative tax burden allow for a few crude generalizations. Census of government finances data on per-capita tax revenues compare Hawaii to the other 49 states and the District of Columbia. Hawaii ranks number one (highest) in per-capita taxes on sales and gross receipts (excise taxes), number five in per-capita general revenues raised by state and local governments, number six in per-capita tax revenues, number seven in per-capita income-tax revenues, and number 39 in per-capita property taxes. At the same time, Hawaii is fourteenth in per-capita total state and local government expenditures.

Tourists' impact. How does one interpret these results? First, the high level of excise-tax receipts reflects both a potent tax system and the presence of tourists, who have a high propensity to spend. Per-capita excise tax revenues are especially high in Hawaii because taxes paid by tourists are taken into account, but the tourists themselves are not (the denominator is "number of residents"). With or without tourists, however, the comprehensive coverage of Hawaii's excise taxes creates an unusually high burden for residents.

Second, Hawaii's relatively high ranking in terms of the per-capita income-tax burden is a direct product of Hawaii's exceptionally high marginal income-tax rates and the cumulative impact of inflation (which through time pushes families into higher tax brackets). Changes in 1987 and 1989 that reduced the number of marginal tax brackets helped offset the base broadening and other effects of the federal Tax Reform Act of 1986 (TRA 86). These changes were touted locally as tax reductions, but really did no more than adjust for what otherwise would have been an inadvertent increase in state income taxes. The fact that the State initially resisted the temptation to rake in the TRA 86 "windfall"—the increase in state taxes resulting from federal tax-law changes—is good but, without further restructuring, it will eventually get a "windfall" anyway. In other words, income taxes in Hawaii are high now and are poised to increase without fanfare or vote.

Political football. Third, Hawaii's relatively low ranking in per-capita property-tax revenues reflects two contradictory aspects of taxes at the county level. Hawaii's notoriously high real estate values mean that lower property-tax rates are still capable of generating relatively high revenues. In repeated concessions to populist sentiment, however, property tax rates have been gradually lowered as property values have risen. Thus, the potential of the property-tax system as a revenue-generating mechanism has been allowed gradually to erode for short-term political gain, to the long-term detriment of tax collections. Perversely, those with the most wealth in the form of real property have benefitted the most from these tax changes. To add insult to the injury of increased regressivity, these property tax rate reductions have also diminished the tax system's ability to generate revenues from foreign investors, property owners notorious for their ability to circumvent other forms of taxation.

Fourth, the fact that Hawaii ranks fifth in per-capita general revenues collected from its own sources, but ranks fourteenth in per-capita general expenditures, suggests the extent to which Hawaii's residents are "not getting their money's worth." Because the presence

of large numbers of tourists requires commensurate public services to be directed at this *de facto* population component (not to mention government subsidies for tourism), Hawaii's residents get even less for their money. Other states that depend on large sources of external income generally are able to manage a level of per-capita government expenditure in line with their higher per-capita tax burdens. In a way, Hawaii's statistics suggest a "loaves and fishes" story, in reverse.

Fifth, even if one is inclined to throw out the rankings altogether, a look at the absolute levels of per-capita taxation leads to the same conclusion. The tax burden for fiscal 1989 was $4,897.20 per capita in Hawaii, 12 percent higher than the $4,368.77 nationwide average. Sophisticated studies suggest that the cost of government in Hawaii should be about equal to the national average, despite our high cost of living. Consequently, unless Hawaii residents are receiving a level or quality of public services 12 percent above the national norm, taxes in Hawaii are too high.

Finally, the most recent Hawaii State Tax Review Commission, after hundreds of hours of study and discussion, and based upon the reports of many consultants, put the following right at the top of its long list of recommendations: "In the aggregate, Hawaii's state taxes are being maintained at a higher level than necessary to fund current policy initiatives. Given the constitutional spending ceiling, the overall level of taxes could be lowered." In other words, if the State intends to adhere to the spirit of the constitutional spending ceiling, taxes are "too high."

CHAPTER 14

TOURIST TAXES

JAMES MAK
Professor of Economics
University of Hawaii

"Are we overtaxing tourists?"

That certainly was the opinion of a tourist whose complaints were printed by a Honolulu newspaper in 1992. She was especially upset about having to pay a $2 daily tax on her rental car. Interestingly, her letter did not mention that she was taxed *twice* on her use of that car; she also had to pay a 4 percent (actually 4.16 percent) excise tax on her car rental. What probably irked her was that she didn't pay the $2 daily tax the previous time she came to Hawaii. This particular tax took effect in 1992.

She was taxed twice on her hotel room as well. Her hotel bill showed a 4.16 percent excise tax and a 5 percent (actually 5.25 percent) transient accommodation tax, for a combined rate of nearly 9.5 percent on the price of the room. The hotel room tax went into effect in 1987 and now generates about $80 million a year in tax revenues.

The unhappy tourist also paid 4.16 percent on just about everything else she bought while in Hawaii—services as well as goods—just like residents. But taxes on items such as car and hotel rentals are intentionally discriminatory. They were enacted with the understanding that the lion's share of those taxes would be paid by tourists. (Don't ask for the exact percentage, because no one knows for sure!)

In addition to the taxes levied directly on her purchases, our already-irate tourist paid a lot of taxes hidden in the price of everything she bought. For example, some of the property tax paid by the owner of her hotel no doubt showed up in the hotel room rate she paid. In Honolulu and Maui counties, the highest property tax rates are levied on hotels. In Honolulu, the 1991 tax rate on hotels was nearly triple the rate paid by homeowners and owners of apartments that are rented out to nontourists. Hotels do their best to pass along these higher taxes.

Similarly, when the restaurant she frequented bought food from a local wholesale grocer, it paid an excise tax; that tax was then passed along to her, not separately stated, but hidden in the price of the meal she ate.

When all taxes are taken into account, tourists directly and indirectly account for more than one out of every five dollars of state and county tax revenues, despite the fact that only one out of every eight people in Hawaii on any given day is a tourist.

Tourists don't vote. Hawaii is not the only state to levy taxes on tourists. Indeed, tourist taxes have become the rage in state and local public finance. The reason is simple. Since 1979, federal financial support for state and local governments has fallen dramatically. At the same time, federally mandated programs have imposed new financial responsibilities. Caught between falling resources and rising responsibilities, state and local governments have been looking desperately for new money to maintain public services. It can be difficult to cut services, and political suicide to raise taxes on residents. The politically "easy" answer is to hit the tourist. Tourists don't vote ... except with their feet. As long as not too many of them are chased away by exorbitant taxes, lots of new tax revenues can be generated without anyone getting voted out of office.

The darling of all tourist taxes is the hotel room tax, now levied virtually everywhere in the United States by local government, state government, or both. A survey of large U.S. cities during the mid-1980s found that the median hotel room tax rate was about 7 percent; by 1990 the median was 10 percent, an increase of some 40 percent. Thus, Hawaii's combined hotel room tax of nearly 9.5 percent is about average.

Are we gouging tourists when we levy taxes that fall primarily on them? Not necessarily. Since tourists don't pay our state income tax,

94

we have to figure other ways for them to help pay for the cost of govern-ment generally, not to mention police, highways, beaches and parks.

Two studies done in the 1970s concluded that tourists in Hawaii paid more in taxes than they got back in the form of public services. Based on those studies, some tourism industry officials argue that tourists are paying more than their fair share of taxes. That's certainly one criterion for fairness, but it's not the only one. For example, few would rate the fairness of our state and federal tax systems by comparing what each one of us pays in taxes against what we receive in services. Indeed, I would be surprised to find many people who know exactly how much they are paying in federal or state and local taxes, or how to begin to calculate the value of what they are getting in return. Besides, it would be impossible to measure what tourists do get as a result of the taxes they pay.

"Tax to da max." The economic rationale for taxing tourists does not rest on equating taxes paid with services received; that much is clear. But on what basis are they taxed?

The goal should be to maximize the state's economic benefits from tourism. It may sound terrible to the tourist, but this boils down to taxing them as much as they will bear.

Tourism consumes substantial resources of this state and contrib-utes to the deterioration of the environment and the quality of residents' lives. Many benefit directly from tourism, but most do not. Tourist taxes are a form of compensation to all the residents of Hawaii, including those who do not otherwise benefit from their presence. Hawaii is not alone in taking this tack.

In Nevada, tourism directly accounts for more than half of all state tax revenues. Political leaders in that state make no bones about their goal of getting as much revenue from tourists as possible.

It is common practice among nontourist-oriented states to design their tax systems to maximize economic benefits to their own residents. Often, they do it by levying special taxes on goods that they sell in particularly large quantities to non-resident buyers. To the extent that these taxes are passed on to out-of-state consumers and producers, there is a transfer of income to residents who are the better off for it. Alaska gets most of its tax revenues from the oil industry. Wyoming gets large amounts from mining. The Pacific Northwest states generate sizable

"RESERVATIONS...FOR FOUR ?... I HAVE NOTHING 'TILL NEXT TUESDAY...,"

tax revenues from the timber industry. If you think of tourism as the primary export of states like Hawaii and Nevada, it is easy to see that tourist taxes have much in common with these other taxes.

There's a limit. Of course, it's possible to go too far. Just as car manufacturing companies could move from Michigan if that state were to impose a burdensome tax on them alone, tourists can choose to stay away if taxation makes vacations in Hawaii too expensive. If this happens, taxation actually reduces the net societal benefits from tourism.

Taking each of Hawaii's tourist taxes separately, it is possible to make a strong case for each one. However, we should ask: when we take all the taxes levied on tourists together, are we gouging them to the point that many will, for that reason, stay home? I say no. Taxes levied on our hotel rooms are not particularly high compared to those levied in competing destinations. Hawaii's hotel room rates, inclusive of taxes, have always been competitive. Car rental rates continue to be low in comparison to numerous other vacation destinations in the Pacific or on the Mainland.

Goods and services are more expensive in Hawaii than elsewhere, but this cannot be attributed primarily to excessive taxes on tourists. It's difficult to argue that we are overtaxing tourists when more come to Hawaii each year than to any other travel destination in the Pacific. Until Operation Desert Storm and the 1991-1992 national recession temporarily slowed the flow, the number of tourists coming to Hawaii kept rising each year, despite the imposition of new taxes.

As for the future, a greater threat to the health of the tourist industry in Hawaii is *too many* tourists. Chasing them away with high taxes may be the least of our problems. The bottom line is that Hawaii still offers good value, despite its new tourist taxes. To our tourist friends I say, "Lucky you vacation Hawaii!"

CHAPTER 15

TAXING RETIREMENT INCOME

JACK P. SUYDERHOUD

Professor of Decision Sciences
College of Business Administration
University of Hawaii

"Is it true that retirees pay no state income tax on their retirement income?"

A quick, simple answer is "yes." Before I explain, however, let me ask a multiple-choice question.

When the president of a large Hawaii corporation retires on a great big pension, will he or she be able to:

A.   Play golf at Waialae Country Club every day instead of just twice a week.

B.   Use his or her yacht more often.

C.   Pay zero income taxes to the State of Hawaii.

D.   Receive an annual welfare check from the State of Hawaii.

E.   All of the above.

Remarkably, the answer could be "E. All of the above." This is so because Hawaii is a great place for golfing and boating *and* because it is one of only two states that exempts all pension and Social Security income from state income taxes. Our retired executive can receive unlimited income from such sources, pay no state income tax, and qualify to receive a "welfare" check in the form of refundable tax credits. With the help of an aggressive tax advisor, a clever person of any age may be able to receive tax-free "pension" benefits from his or her controlled corporation. The law is remarkably ambiguous, and it is common knowledge among tax experts that aggressive planning in this area generally works by default.

The rationale. Since most working people pay a significant portion of their income to the state tax collector, it is reasonable for them to ask why this special treatment is provided to *all* who receive pension income. After all, sooner or later every tax break gets paid for by other taxpayers.

Just before statehood, the territorial government studied the potential for attracting well-off retired people to live in Hawaii as a way of fostering economic development. There is no documentary evidence that the income-tax preferences for retirement income are related to that effort. However, some argue that they are necessary to keep Hawaii attractive as a retirement location, especially for federal civilian and military retirees.

For the most part, however, the tax preferences are rationalized on the basis of the economic needs of the elderly. As a group, the elderly have made many positive contributions to our society and deserve respect. Many are burdened by ever-increasing medical costs and some lack the funds to meet basic needs.

It is a popular stereotype that all the elderly are poor and live on a fixed income. As is the case for most stereotypes, this is far from the truth.

Elderly aren't so poor. As a whole, the elderly are no poorer than the rest of the adult population. According to the U.S. Census Bureau, the 1989 income per U.S. household member was essentially the same for households with elderly ($13,345) and without ($13,978). Another study found that the proportion of elderly living in poverty fell significantly from 1970 to 1982, to the point where the elderly, as a group, had lower poverty rates than any other age group. Nevertheless, myths about the elderly always being poor persist, and Hawaii's special treatment of pension income is built largely upon this myth.

For better or worse, let's consider the federal income tax as a benchmark. Pension income generally is fully taxable, and 50 percent of social security benefits are taxable for single taxpayers with income above $25,000 or joint filers with income above $32,000. While most states have special rules affecting the elderly, of all states that have income taxes Hawaii is the most generous in its treatment of retirement income. All income from pensions (whether public or private) and all social security benefits are excluded for tax purposes. The pension income of someone living in California, for example, is fully taxable, the same as any other type of income.

In Hawaii, a taxpayer doesn't have to report retirement income. The tax forms don't even have a space for it. Naturally, this encourages aggressive taxpayers to take extreme positions with respect to the definition of "pensions" and "retirement." Many tax advisors argue that a person does not have to be elderly or stop working to "retire." Even the State Department of Taxation agrees that "pension" benefits can be received in one lump sum and still qualify for special treatment.

Tax exemptions. In addition to the exclusion of pension income, Hawaii provides a double exemption—an extra $1,040 per exemption in 1991—for elderly taxpayers, thereby further reducing taxable income. Since Hawaii has some of the highest state income-tax rates in the nation (up to 10 percent), the value of these exclusions and exemptions can be considerable.

The exclusion of pension and social security income means that the State is not collecting as much revenue as it otherwise would. Unlike the federal government which can borrow to make up for revenue shortfalls, the State must raise taxes elsewhere when it provides tax breaks to select groups. Based on research done in 1989 for the Hawaii State Tax Review Commission, retirement income exclusions reduce state income tax collections by about 5 percent. That amounted to about $35 million in 1990. Stated another way, the exclusions cost every tax filer about $100 in additional income taxes.

The retirement income preferences have other insidious effects, especially with respect to our sense of fairness. It is widely held that taxes, as distasteful as they are, should at least be fair. For the income tax, fairness is usually defined in the following way: those with equal incomes should pay roughly equal taxes. The retirement income preference insures this will not be the case.

In Table 1, Hawaii income-tax liabilities are calculated for three hypothetical households, all with the same gross income. Household A has two wage earners whose combined income is $40,000 a year (before taxes) and two children. (Don't ask how they can survive.) Household B is a retired couple with $17,000 in Social Security benefits and $23,000 of interest and dividend income from investments made before retiring. Household C also is a retired couple who together have $17,000 in Social Security benefits plus pension income of $23,000 per year.

Working family pays. The working family, Household A, must pay the State $1,843 in income taxes. The retirees of Household B are unfortunate enough to receive the majority of their retirement income from interest and dividends. This income is taxable. But, because of the exclusion of the Social Security benefits, plus the availability of refundable credits, they pay only a small tax—$158. The retirees of Household C, in contrast, with the same $40,000 in gross income, *receive* a $1,050 check from the State because none of their income is taxable and they qualify for refundable tax credits.

This violates basic standards of equity. All three families in the hypothetical example have $40,000 income, but only the working couple pays a significant tax and Household C actually receives a substantial payment from the State. Effectively, we penalize workers and retirees whose income is from interest and dividends in favor of those with pensions. And this doesn't even consider the possibility that Household C's "pension" is the result of clever tax planning.

You might argue that the elderly deserve special treatment, and I agree that some of the elderly do deserve tax preferences. However, not all people receiving pension income are elderly and not all need tax relief. In 1989, 37 percent of all pension income received by Hawaii residents went to taxpayers with an adjusted gross income (AGI) of more than $50,000 and almost two-thirds went to those with an AGI over $30,000. By excluding all pension income from the tax base, the "well-off" retired actually benefit much more than the "elderly poor."

Making it fairer. Our state income tax would be fairer if the tax relief currently provided to "retired" taxpayers were instead targeted at the poor (whether working or retired). This could be accomplished by adopting the same approach as the federal income tax. However, this means virtually all pension income would be taxable. A less severe approach would be to do what many other states do: exempt only a certain amount of pension income from the tax, say, the first $10,000 per elderly person. Another way of increasing fairness would be to count all forms of income, including retirement, to determine eligibility for credits and credit amounts.

These suggestions are consistent with the notion that an income tax is fair if it taxes income the same way, regardless of the source. They also are consistent with the notion that a tax base should allow few exclusions so that rates can be kept low. For a number of good reasons, tax relief can and should be provided to the poor. By carefully targeting income-tax relief, we can afford to provide more relief to those who really need it and keep taxes on everyone else as low as possible. Plus, we can avoid the ridiculous situation of a retired corporate executive qualifying for low-income tax credits.

Table 1
HAWAII INCOME TAX LIABILITIES OF
THREE HYPOTHETICAL HOUSEHOLDS, 1990

	Household A (working family)	Household B (retired couple with interest income)	Household C (retired couple with pension income)
Gross Income	$40,000	$40,000	$40,000
Adj. Gross Income	$40,000	$23,000*	$0 **
Less standard deductions and exemptions	$ 6,060	$ 6,060	$6,060
Taxable income	$33,940	$16,940	($6,060)
Tax from tax table	$ 2,503	$ 1,028	$0
Total credits ***	$ 600	$ 870	$ 1,050
Net tax liability	$ 1,843	$ 158	($1,050)

* Only $23,000 interest and dividend income is taxable. $17,000 Social Security income is exempt.
** $23,000 pension income and $17,000 Social Security income are exempt.
*** Includes food tax, excise tax, low income renter, general income tax and medical services credits.

" . . . the imposition of an excise tax on interbusiness transactions . . . violates principles of equity and efficiency . . . [this tax] is hidden from the consumers who ultimately pay it in the form of higher prices on goods and services." **Hawaii State Tax Review Commission**

CHAPTER 16

EXCISE TAXES

WILLIAM F. FOX

(Formerly UH Visiting Professor of Economics)
Professor of Economics
University of Tennessee

"Is it true that Hawaii would need a 20 percent sales tax to generate the same revenue it gets from a 4 percent excise tax?"

A Hawaii State Tax Review Commission reached that conclusion in the mid-1980s. I think 16 percent is closer, but even that would seem shockingly high to most people.

Technically, both sales and excise taxes are on transactions. However, it's best to think of them as taxes on consumption. Experts generally agree that a well-designed system will tax income, wealth and consumption on a roughly equal basis, that is, one-third of total revenues from each source. The basic idea is to spread the pain, and to keep rates as low as possible.

Hawaii residents pay unusually high taxes on income and consumption, and unusually low taxes on wealth. The most distinguishing characteristic of Hawaii's system, however, is the potency of its excise tax. Comparing a conventional sales tax to Hawaii's excise tax is a bit like comparing a firecracker to a hand grenade.

105

We apply the 4 percent excise tax rate to an amazingly broad base. The implications of this are interesting. For example, in most states the sales tax rate is higher than 4 percent. But the resulting revenue, as a percentage of statewide personal income, averages only 2.3 percent nationally. In only two mainland states does this percentage exceed 4 percent. Hawaii's recently was 5.8 percent!

Revenues per person tell the same story. Hawaii's $1,057 per person is much greater than the per-capita sales tax revenue collected by any other state, including states that like Hawaii shift a sizable portion of total taxes to nonresidents.

The phenomenal productivity of our excise tax has resulted in a dependence on it as a revenue source. The excise tax contributed 50.4 percent of Hawaii's total tax revenues in 1990. On the average, other states get 33.1 percent of their revenues from their sales tax.

Tax all transactions. The excise "tax base," used in measuring the potency of the tax, is calculated by dividing the amount collected by the tax rate. Many mainland experts would consider enactment of a sales tax with a base in excess of 100 percent of statewide personal income to be political suicide. Yet Hawaii's excise tax base is 144.1 percent of personal income—three times the average state's 46.3 percent.

Some of this is attributable to Hawaii's ability to tax tourists and other nonresidents, but most of the difference comes from Hawaii's decision to tax virtually every transaction occurring within the state. Considerable diversity exists, but other states usually exempt sales by certain entities, manufacturers, service providers and wholesalers—all of which are taxable under Hawaii's system. Hawaii does exempt a few entities, including banks and hospitals, but the list is narrow. Also, mainland states often exempt such transactions as the sale of food or payments for property leases, both of which are taxed in Hawaii.

Hawaii's unusually broad tax base has several strong advantages. First, it permits Hawaii to raise more revenue than other states while using a relatively modest tax rate. Low rates are normally preferred because they are less likely to cause people or businesses to change their behavior to avoid the tax or evade payment. Plus, it looks good politically. Second, the broad base is more likely to result in horizontal equity, which means that people with the same level of consumption pay the same tax. In many states, sales tax liability depends as much on what you consume as on how much you consume.

Shortcomings. Hawaii's excise tax is not perfect. The relationship between a household's income and its tax payments is normally referred to as vertical equity. In this regard the excise tax is regressive; as household income rises, tax payments fall as a percentage of that income. The most important reason is that households are able to save more as they earn higher incomes.

Many in Hawaii believe that a progressive income tax (one in which tax payments as a percentage of household income rise, as income rises) is important for offsetting the regressivity of the excise tax. This is the primary justification for the excise-tax credit available to Hawaii residents when they file state income tax returns.

It's OK for one component of a state's tax system to be regressive as long as other components offset that to a significant degree. When Hawaii's progressive income tax is combined with its regressive excise tax, the overall tax burden is only mildly regressive. Hawaii's tax system is quite progressive compared to those of other states (in other words, most states have a tax system that is significantly more regressive than Hawaii's).

Pyramiding. Another shortcoming of Hawaii's excise tax is the potential for pyramiding because the tax is imposed at each stage of the production process. The total tax rate incorporated in the final price is greater than the legislated rate. For example, suppose a parcel of property is leased for $1,000 and subsequently subleased two times, each after a 10 percent markup. This is not uncommon in Hawaii. The total excise tax on leasing this property would be more than 14 percent of the initial lease rent. A tenant next door could be paying a mere 4 percent. That seems unfair.

Pyramiding can be a problem for a variety of other reasons. First, it encourages tax evasion. In the leasing example, there is an incentive to hide the subleases. A general rule is that tax evasion rises with the effective tax rate. Second, people will tend to buy fewer goods and services where the tax pyramids most. People may be worse off when their consumption choices are altered, and heavily taxed businesses are at a competitive disadvantage. Third, pyramiding can change the way businesses operate. A manufacturer typically would be taxed upon selling a product to a wholesaler, who is then taxed upon selling it to the retailer, who is then taxed as the product finally is sold to the consumer. These three levels of tax can be reduced to one if the manufacturer buys the wholesaler and the retailer, and thereafter sells directly to the consumer. Thus, a pyramiding tax tends to work to the disadvantage of small or new businesses.

For the most part, however, pyramiding is less onerous than might be expected. One study found that the effective tax rate on average consumption expenditures in Hawaii was "only" 5.3 percent. The main reason it wasn't higher is that sales by manufacturers and wholesalers are taxed at 0.5 percent, unless the sale is considered to be at retail, so usually the pyramiding is of a 0.5 percent tax. Also, our economy may be less complex than that of other states in that goods and services go through fewer stages of production (although a less complex economy partly could be the product of efforts to avoid the tax). In any event, fewer stages of production mean less pyramiding.

Politicians love it. Politicians love the excise tax (once it is in place) because it raises so much revenue without ruffling too many feathers. First of all, most voters who compare mainland sales tax rates to Hawaii's 4 percent excise tax feel pretty good about it. You now know that is like comparing apples to a watermelon. Second, unlike property taxes that get paid in two big installments each year (ouch, that hurts) or income taxes that get added up on an annual return (wow, I can't believe I pay that much), consumers seldom pay a large excise tax at one time and almost never add up the total for the year. How much in excise taxes did you pay last year? See what I mean?

Mainland politicians covet Hawaii's excise tax. Slowly but surely, virtually every state with a sales tax is considering adjustments to make it more like our excise tax. Well-financed groups lobby loudly against such changes and thus far have been more successful than not. For example, 1987 Florida legislation put a wide range of services under its sales tax, but lobbying pressure led to repeal after only six months. Florida is again considering taxation of services, but this time more narrowly selected. Most other states also want to tax a broader set of goods and services, but thus far they have experienced only piecemeal success.

Hawaii politicians especially like the fact that nonresidents pay roughly 30 percent of total excise taxes. It's called tax exporting. Interestingly, the few studies that have been done on tax exporting in

Hawaii indicate that our property tax is an even more effective vehicle.

I have commented on the regressivity of our excise tax, the fact that it pyramids, that it is largely a hidden tax, and that it's not necessarily best for tax exporting. Does that mean I think radical changes are in order? It may surprise you to find that I do not. Even with its flaws, Hawaii's excise tax is a good tax, in need of nothing more than fine tuning and, perhaps, a rate reduction. It ain't perfect, but it ain't broke either. In a world where all taxes are flawed in one way or another, as long as the rate is kept as low as possible, Hawaii's excise tax looks pretty good to me.

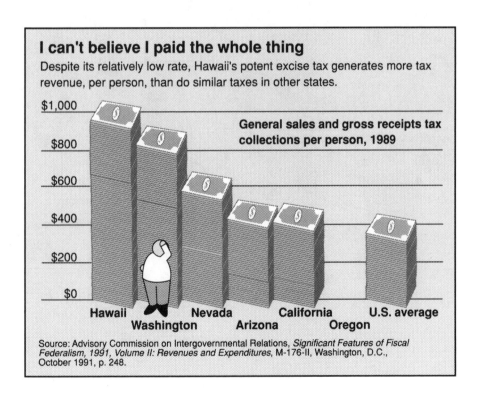

I can't believe I paid the whole thing

Despite its relatively low rate, Hawaii's potent excise tax generates more tax revenue, per person, than do similar taxes in other states.

General sales and gross receipts tax collections per person, 1989

Hawaii   Nevada   California   U.S. average
Washington   Arizona   Oregon

Source: Advisory Commission on Intergovernmental Relations, *Significant Features of Fiscal Federalism, 1991, Volume II: Revenues and Expenditures*, M-176-II, Washington, D.C., October 1991, p. 248.

"HERE COMES THE AMBULANCE CHASER..."

CHAPTER 17

TAXING FOOD & MEDICAL CARE

WILLIAM F. FOX
(Formerly UH Visiting Professor of Economics)
Professor of Economics
University of Tennessee

"Why should people have to pay a 4 percent excise tax on groceries and medical care?"

Forty-five states, including Hawaii, have a sales tax. Most of them exempt food purchased for consumption at home. But all food is taxed in Hawaii, and only Hawaii and New Mexico do not exempt most medical care.

Many people have criticized the fact that food and medical care are taxed in Hawaii. After all, food is a basic necessity, and it just doesn't seem right that people's medical misfortune would increase their tax burden. Quite frankly, it initially seemed rather heartless that Hawaii would tax food and medical care. A closer look, however, leads to a different conclusion.

Broad base. Hawaii's excise tax has many positive characteristics. Perhaps at the top of the list is the fact that it can generate so much revenue with such a low rate. It has a very broad base; practically nothing is exempt. The arguments for including food and health care in the excise tax base are the arguments for a broad base.

If food and medical care were exempted, many decisions by the legislature, department of taxation, and vendors would be necessary as to what qualifies as "food" and "medical care." For example, would membership in a health spa qualify as "medical care"? Could it ever? If you think that sounds silly, try writing a set of instructions that others could use to clearly and consistently distinguish medical care from other expenditures. Would "food" include chewing gum, dog food and soft drinks? Other states' efforts to deal with questions like these often are laughable. For example, in New York small marshmallows and plain peanuts are exempt, but big marshmallows and chocolate covered peanuts are taxable. If the exemption applies only to food for consumption at home (as is the case in most "exempt" states), is a salad bar at the grocery store taxable? The list of questions goes on and on.

Most studies have demonstrated that vendors make many mistakes because of ever-growing complexity, and take increasingly aggressive positions because of inherent ambiguity. From the State's standpoint, an exemption can be terribly difficult and expensive to administer. Ignore it and vendors develop a cynical attitude about "collecting" and paying the tax; actively police it and the cost quickly becomes burdensome.

More advantages. A broad-based sales tax is more likely to be horizontally equitable, meaning people with the same consumption will pay the same tax. A broad tax base requires people to bear the same tax burden if they spend the same amount of money, regardless of whether they get a face lift (medical care?), purchase gourmet food from a deli (food for home consumption?), or buy a new car (clearly something we want to tax). A household's tax burden should be determined by how much it buys, not what it buys.

Economists like the fact that a broad-based tax has less effect on what people buy. The tax does not influence a person's decision between going out to dinner or going to a movie as long as both are taxed, although the tax does reduce the amount available to spend on either option. Taxes are the cost of civilization and therefore necessary, but they should not make businesses compete on a tilted playing field.

Finally, and very importantly, a broad tax base allows a lower tax rate. This has many advantages, including that it discourages evasion. It may sound simplistic, but a low rate is probably the single most important component of a "good" tax.

The other side. The major argument for exempting food is to achieve greater equity. One estimate is that people earning less than $10,000 a year pay more than 4 percent of their income in excise taxes while those earning more than $40,000 pay less than 2 percent. Low-income people purchase more food relative to their income, so exemption of food would lessen the overall regressivity of the excise tax. Similar arguments might be made for exempting health care because many low-income people need relatively more medicines and medical supplies. Prescription medicine already is exempt from the excise tax.

Some health care services are provided by not-for-profit hospitals and agencies. However, this is not an acceptable reason for exemption since the tax is intended to be passed forward to the consumer.

Stalemate. Unfortunately, we seem to have a stalemate. Exemption of food and health care may improve one concept of fairness (the relative tax burden borne by high-income versus low-income people), but it does so at the expense of simplicity, efficiency and one aspect of equity (that people with the same consumption should pay the same taxes). Even proponents of a food and medical care exemption recognize it as a poor way of targeting low-income people for assistance. Low-income people might receive the greatest percentage reduction in their tax burden from exemption, but high income people would save more in absolute tax dollars. Consequently, most of the tax savings would not go to the intended group.

Fortunately, Hawaii has adopted a means of balancing all the competing concerns. Food and medical care are kept in the excise tax base, and the resulting problems are addressed by giving credits against the income tax. This approach implicitly assumes that equity is best achieved by ensuring that the burden of all taxes (as opposed to each tax) is fair. Addressing equity through the overall tax system, as Hawaii does, is a reasonable approach.

The credit approach enables the State to enjoy the benefits of a broad excise tax base and yet offset the resulting regressivity in a way that is simple and theoretically efficient. The cost of improving equity, in terms of lost tax revenues, is lower because equity is achieved by giving relatively more of the benefits to the target group. As a bonus, the broader-based excise tax is collected from both residents and nonresidents, but only residents receive the income tax credits.

Politicians sometimes are accused of taking stands calculated to gain them votes, even if those stands are flawed. With respect to the exemption of food and medical care from the excise tax, however, the State has taken an enlightened approach despite the fact that most voters probably do not understand this area well enough to appreciate its beauty. But that does not mean the current approach cannot be improved.

Ways to improve. Tax credits for food bear no direct relationship to actual excise-tax payments. They are a means of directly increasing the progressivity of the income tax, not of directly reducing the regressivity of the excise tax. Labeling credits invites lobbying for a host of other specific credits. Consequently, a single income-tax credit for low-income individuals, without any explicit attempt to tie it to the excise tax, would be an excellent way to improve tax equity in Hawaii.

Hawaii's medical credits are linked to actual excise tax payments, so they directly reduce its burden and lessen its regressivity. They probably fail to achieve their intended purpose, however, since there is an upper limit to the tax credit. It does not help a person with a catastrophic illness any more than someone with a relatively minor ailment. A preferred medical credit would be one allowed only where unusually high medical costs are incurred. In other words, the opposite of what we have now.

Low-income people must file a return to receive the benefit of credits, but a significant number do not file. State tax officials must better inform low-income residents of the potential benefits of filing state income-tax returns.

The current approach of taxing food and medical care makes sense and is anything but heartless. If the people of Hawaii want a reduction in the amount of excise taxes they pay, it makes more sense simply to lower the tax rate than it does to exempt specific items.

Not regressive overall

Because of Hawaii's progressive income tax and low-income tax credits, Hawaii's tax burden is much less regressive than that of other states.

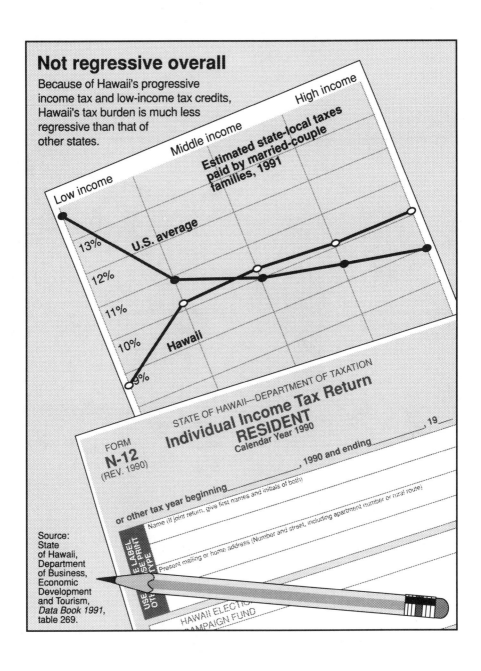

Estimated state-local taxes paid by married-couple families, 1991

Low income   Middle income   High income

13%   U.S. average
12%
11%
10%   **Hawaii**
9%

STATE OF HAWAII—DEPARTMENT OF TAXATION

Individual Income Tax Return
RESIDENT
Calendar Year 1990

FORM
N-12
(REV. 1990)

, 19___

or other tax year beginning_____, 1990 and ending_____

Name (if joint return, give first names and initials of both)

Present mailing or home address (Number and street, including apartment number or rural route)

USE LABEL
PLEASE PRINT
OR TYPE

HAWAII ELECTION
CAMPAIGN FUND

Source:
State
of Hawaii,
Department
of Business,
Economic
Development
and Tourism,
Data Book 1991,
table 269.

CHAPTER 18

PROPERTY TAXES

RANDALL W. ROTH

Professor of Law
William S. Richardson School of Law
University of Hawaii

"Should property taxes be reduced?"

No tax is popular, but national surveys indicate the property tax is particularly unpopular. Ironically, there is much to be said in its favor.

A good tax apparatus will generate a stable cash flow for government, have little impact on taxpayers' economic decisions and be equitable in the sense that people in similar situations pay similar amounts. Relative to other possibilities, an annual tax on property values fits this description reasonably well.

There's more. The property tax is relatively easy to administer, and compliance costs are remarkably low. Perhaps most important of all, most experts rate it high on the "fairness" scale. Here's why:

First, per capita differences in county tax bases tend to be larger under either an income tax or a consumption tax. In plain English, this means the property tax is relatively good at smoothing out the differences between "rich" counties and "poor" counties.

Second, to the extent it is a tax on housing consumption, it generally falls evenly across income classes. That is, it tends to be a proportionate tax on housing consumption. Better yet, as a tax on investment property it tends to be disproportionately borne by high-income individuals. A tax that is partly proportionate and partly progressive seems fairer than other possible sources of county revenue which tend to be regressive.

Third, because the property tax is highly visible, taxpayers are especially likely to hold government accountable for sensible use of the money. Governments tend to function best when taxpayers are vigilant.

Fourth, property taxes satisfy the "benefit principle." That is, the correlation between taxes paid and benefit received tends to be relatively high. Local services, such as police, fire protection and roads are basically site-oriented—they benefit property owners by protecting or increasing their property values. The importance of this benefit principle cannot be overstated.

Helpful assumptions. Not convinced? OK, let's approach your question from a completely different direction. To do so, we must make several assumptions. The first is that the total amount of all taxes—on income, sales, property, gas, etc.—currently collected in Hawaii by state and county governments is neither too high nor too low. The second: state and county governments have been combined into one giant Hawaii Government that receives all taxes and provides all government services. This second assumption will help us deal separately with the fact that public schools in Hawaii are not funded through the property tax.

A good state-wide tax system will include more than just one source of revenue. Multiple sources make possible a stable flow of revenue with lower rates, better compliance and a relatively level playing field. As a result, much can be said in support of having Hawaii Government tax more than just income, more than just sales and more than just property. (Remember, the level of total taxes is not yet an issue here.)

Given these assumptions, if property taxes were to be eliminated, the revenue loss would have to be made up elsewhere. This generally would mean that income and/or excise taxes of renters (among others) would have to go up so that homeowners' and investors' property taxes could come down. Does that sound fair?

It has been estimated that a greater percentage of total property taxes—as compared to income and excise taxes—is borne by nonresidents. Calculation of the percentage of any particular tax ultimately borne by nonresidents ("exported") is an inexact process. Nevertheless, three separate studies have pegged the export rate for the property tax within a few points of 40 percent. Other studies have calculated an approximately 30 percent export rate for the excise tax. The rate for the income tax has been put at less than 20 percent. If these studies are accurate, a shift in reliance from property taxes to income or excise taxes would result in a reduction in the amount of taxes exported. Also, income and excise taxes can be avoided by foreign investors (legally and illegally) more easily than property taxes. Do you really want to shift taxes from nonresidents to residents and make it easier for foreign investors to avoid paying Hawaii taxes?

Inflated property values. Perhaps by now you are thinking that the property tax is not all bad, but you wonder if it makes sense to base the property tax on market values when those amounts are so greatly inflated.

The property taxes you pay are based on two factors: assessed value and tax rate. It makes no sense to complain about property taxes solely on the basis of high assessed values. For example, if some mainland state with low property values were to increase everyone's assessed value tenfold, but simultaneously reduce everyone's tax rate by the same factor of ten, the taxes paid by each property owner in that state would remain unchanged. Would their taxes now be oppressive because of the high assessed values of their properties? Obviously not.

Some residents in high-priced areas of Hawaii complain that the market values of their homes were "puffed up" disproportionately by purchases (primarily by foreign investors) during the late 1980s and early 1990s. Arguing that most of this run-up in value was artificial and of no immediate benefit to them, they contend that the assessed value of their homes should never go up by more than some fixed, islandwide rate. Examples of older people being forced to sell their homes in order to pay property taxes sometimes are cited. (The counties provide extra exemptions based on age, but these are of limited benefit to homeowners in particularly high-value areas.)

California's "Proposition 13" approach of limiting annual increases in assessed value to an artificially low percentage (until the property is sold, at which time the assessed value is set at market value) benefits existing homeowners, but increases the burden of other taxpayers generally and future home buyers in particular. A Hawaii homeowners group has promoted a Hawaii version. Though legal, this approach inevitably would lead to unfair distinctions and should not be pursued. One critic of Proposition 13 has publicly identified a $2.1 million beach-front property in Malibu with an assessed value equal to that of his own recently purchased $170,000 home in Baldwin Hills. Does that sound fair?

Targeted relief. The counties easily could develop additional relief mechanisms for targeted homeowners who can no longer afford to pay property taxes. Such relief could take any number of forms, the most logical of which would be a "circuit breaker" that limits property tax liability to a maximum percentage of a homeowner's income. A growing number of jurisdictions on the Mainland take a different approach. They give homeowners the option of letting unpaid taxes accumulate, at interest, until the owner's death. In effect, the government thereby gets into the home equity loan business, using money provided by other taxpayers. The point is that relief easily can be targeted to deserving individuals. The fact that some property owners need relief is a separate issue from the overall level of property taxes.

Interesting comparisons. You might find it interesting to compare the level of property taxes in Hawaii to those of other states. In 1990, per-capita property taxes were $384 in Hawaii. This was quite low compared to the U.S. average of $626. Similarly, property taxes per $1,000 of personal income were quite low in Hawaii ($20.72) compared to the U.S. average ($35.62).

A Coldwell Banker survey in January 1990 compared prices and property taxes on a "standard executive home" (2,200 square feet with four bedrooms, two-and-one-half baths, family room and two-car garage in a neighborhood typical for corporate middle management) across the nation. The prices varied from $81,666 in Corpus Christi, Texas, to $916,666 in Beverly Hills, California. The price in Honolulu was $438,333. The average of the property taxes actually assessed that year on the Honolulu homes included in the survey was $1,116, far below the national average of $2,507. The Honolulu tax figure was below those of numerous "low cost" cities, including Corpus Christi!

In early 1992, *Money* magazine published the results of a city-by-city property-tax study based on 1991 data. It compared property taxes on a median-value house, as reported in the 1990 Census, in the area

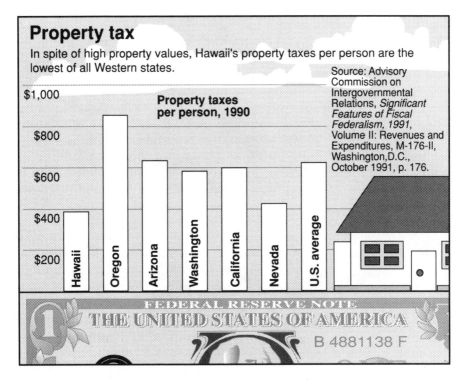

Property tax

In spite of high property values, Hawaii's property taxes per person are the lowest of all Western states.

Property taxes per person, 1990

Source: Advisory Commission on Intergovernmental Relations, *Significant Features of Fiscal Federalism, 1991,* Volume II: Revenues and Expenditures, M-176-II, Washington,D.C., October 1991, p. 176.

of each locale where moderately affluent homeowners (median household income in 1991 of $69,275) were most apt to live. Amounts ranged from zero in a few Louisiana parishes to almost $6,000 in several New Jersey counties. The property tax figure for Honolulu was $830. Specific areas included Salt Lake City ($800), Dallas ($1,250), Miami ($1,300), Sacramento ($1,623), Milwaukee ($2,000), Los Angeles ($2,830), and San Francisco ($3,736). The $830 Honolulu figure was one of the lowest in the study.

No logical connection. Many people argue that everybody's property taxes should be low in Hawaii since they are not used to fund public schools as they often are on the Mainland. This mentality assumes some sort of logical or even necessary connection between property taxes and the financing of public schools. Ironically, many experts question whether the property tax is the most appropriate device for financing public education. Since the mid-1970s the trend on the Mainland has been to substitute state revenues for property taxes to fund public education. Besides, it would make sense to tax wealth

INCOME TAX & EXCISE TAX

Under-utilization of property tax

Property taxes in Hawaii generate an unusually small percentage of total state and local revenues.

PROPERTY TAX SHARE – 1990

25%
20%
15%
10%
5%
0

Hawaii | Oregon | Arizona | Wash. | Calif. | Nevada | U.S. average

Source: Advisory Commission on Intergovernmental Relations.

(along with income and consumption) even if there were no public schools. The counties have required regular cash subsidies from the State in recent years and that money came out of income and excise tax revenues. If property taxes were higher, the State would be in a position to cut income and/or excise taxes.

One can easily argue that Hawaii relies too much on income and excise taxes and not enough on property taxes. In 1990, property taxes contributed only 8.5 percent of total state and county revenue in Hawaii. This was far below the U.S. average of 18.3 percent. Some people don't think it's fair that nonproperty owners have to make up for foregone revenue lost to relatively wealthy property owners.

I have suggested that property taxes are not inherently unfair and that they have been underutilized in Hawaii. Does that mean property taxes should be raised?

The overall level of taxes in Hawaii is extraordinarily high. The public sector is extraordinarily big. Government in Hawaii cannot continue to consume ever-increasing pieces of the economic pie without having it result in smaller and smaller pies. The counties may be underfinanced, and property taxes truly are underutilized, but that does not mean the overall level of taxes in Hawaii should be raised. The degree to which the property tax is underutilized arguably is less than the degree to which the income and excise taxes are overutilized. Keep that in mind as the State tries to get the counties to increase property taxes.

If constituents are alert, they will not argue that property should not be taxed, or even that it should not be taxed more heavily. And they will not be confused by the fact that public education in Hawaii is not financed with property taxes. Instead, they will demand that income and/or excise taxes be reduced by the amount of any property tax increase.

The State is like the magician who wants you to watch the hand labeled "counties." Keep an eye on the other hand, the one labeled "state." It's the one that has your wallet.

CHAPTER 19

PROPERTY TAX FAIRNESS

THOMAS M. FOLEY, ESQ.
Foley Maehara Judge Nip & Chang

"Are property tax assessments even-handed?"

Did you know that the assessed value of some expensive homes in highly desirable Kahala *decreased* in 1992 by 18 percent while that of properties in many less desirable neighborhoods *increased* substantially—some by 30 or 40 percent? Or that identical side-by-side homes sometimes have significantly different assessed values? Do you find it odd that property taxes on Oahu homes have not increased nearly so much as has county spending? Believe it or not, there may be good explanations for these interesting facts.

First, all property in Hawaii—nonresidential as well as residential, improved as well as unimproved—is supposed to be assessed each year based on 100 percent of current market value. Rather than attempting to reappraise each property individually, the counties usually just adjust last year's assessed value, primarily on the basis of sales activity in each neighborhood. The fact that someone's assessed value went up, say, 30 percent suggests that a statistical analysis of recent sales in that neighborhood indicated an increase in market values by roughly that percentage. Overall, assessments in Kahala went up by 5 percent in

1992, but there were areas within Kahala that did indeed drop by 18 percent. The reason is simple: sales activity indicated that market values had actually gone down from the prior year by roughly that percentage.

Second, resident homeowners enjoy a $40,000 exemption in the calculation of property taxes. Additional exemptions are available for older homeowners. The total exemption increases to $60,000 at age 55, $80,000 at 60, $100,000 at 65 and $120,000 once the homeowner reaches 70. Exemptions bring down the net assessed value on which the tax itself is based. Consequently, property owners who use their property as a principal residence enjoy a reduction that is denied to investors. Investors sometime complain that this unfairly shifts more of the total tax burden to them, but not many people lose sleep over it. If government tried to shift the entire burden onto those same shoulders, however, there certainly would be a fairness problem.

Third, it may be that a particular house has been overvalued. Government appraisers are human and sometimes make mistakes. Perhaps an appeal would result in a reduction in the property's assessed value. I suggest that you not get your hopes up, however. Your chances of prevailing are not statistically high. Assessed values tend to "lag" the market by a year or two in any event. Consequently, your property can be overvalued by comparison to other people's properties, and yet be undervalued by comparison to its own current market value. The tax assessor's figure is presumed correct; the burden is on you to show otherwise. Finally, you must show that the assessor was off by more than 10 percent to get any relief. Not surprisingly, few people appeal, and three out of every four taxpayers who do, lose.

Fourth, residential property tax burdens in Hawaii are relatively low, and the trend is downward. Of course, this sounds great to residential property owners. But property tax "relief" that isn't matched by a reduction in county expenditures really just shifts more of the existing burden to others. In the case of Oahu, there certainly hasn't been an expenditure reduction, and the resulting shift of tax burden has been from residential owners to owners of business property.

Shift of burden on Oahu. From 1984 to 1991, the average annual increase in real property tax revenue from improved residential property was only 1.6 percent, but was 13.5 percent on commercial property and 18.1 percent on hotel/resort property. A 1991 study by the

Honolulu Real Property Tax Advisory Committee showed the share of total property tax revenues raised from residential properties declined from 46.95 percent in fiscal 1987-88 to 31.74 percent in fiscal 1991-92. That's a whale of a shift.

This dramatic shift has been accomplished in one obvious and one less-than-obvious fashion. The first is through use of "differential tax rates"—separate classes of property taxed at different rates. The 1992 spread was extreme. The hotel/resort rate of $9.64 per $1,000 of assessed value was roughly triple the residential land rate of $3.25 and more than double the residential improvements rate of $4.09.

The less-than-obvious technique for shifting the property tax burden from residential property to business property has to do with valuation. A Honolulu rule directs county appraisers to determine the fair market value of improvements by market data and cost approaches. Consequently, Oahu appraisers ignore how much income a business property is generating, and refuse to consider the possibility that sales of comparable properties to foreign investors might have been for amounts above market value. Business property owners argue that the Honolulu assessment process is unfair because it ignores these important factors.

Several hotels were purchased in the late 1980s and early 1990s at prices far beyond values determined through use of traditional appraisal techniques. These purchases created an aberration within the marketplace and distorted valuations of adjacent and like properties. Commercial properties in downtown Honolulu had similar problems. For example, the 1989 purchase of the Merchandise Mart at Alakea and Hotel streets, at $1,200 per square foot, set a new standard for valuations downtown. Most commercial appraisers regarded that purchase as ill-considered, and yet the county assessor set values in 1990 and 1991 using that isolated sale to dramatically increase other downtown assessed values.

What it all means. Property tax assessments may be evenhanded with respect to property owners within each class, but they are not evenhanded between owners of residential property and owners of business property. This is precisely the sort of thing that gives Hawaii its reputation as a "Tax Hell" for businesses.

CHAPTER 20

BUSINESS TAXES

JACK P. SUYDERHOUD
Professor of Decision Sciences
College of Business Administration
University of Hawaii

"Do businesses pay their fair share of taxes?"

Although asked almost daily, for the most part this is the wrong question. Businesses don't pay taxes; people do. Some of you know instinctively what I mean by that; others will have to read on.

Let's consider a simple and common situation. Wearing your consumer "hat," you go into the hardware store to buy something to fix a dripping sink faucet. The plumbing supplies cost $100, plus $4.16 the hardware store calls a general excise tax, for a total of $104.16. The store owner eventually pays your $4.16 (4 percent of $104.16) to the State. In this simple situation the tax technically was paid by the business, but as a practical matter it was passed on ("shifted") to you, the consumer. This seems like a pretty straight-forward process, but there is much more to it.

The excise tax is only one of many taxes imposed on businesses. If they own or lease the land on which they operate, they must also pay property taxes. In addition, businesses pay taxes on utilities, fuel, insurance premiums, for Social Security, unemployment insurance and on and on. All are called "indirect" taxes. Eventually, they are borne by people as a result of shifting. Since indirect taxes on businesses inevitably are shifted to people, the important question is "which people?"

In life, we wear many hats, often at the same time. We are, for example, consumers, workers, suppliers, creditors and business owners (if not direct owners, then through stocks, mutual funds or pension funds). When a business "pays" a tax, that cost generally is borne by the owners or stockholders (who are also consumers), or shifted to customers or workers. The direction and extent of shifting depends on market conditions. Let's consider several examples.

The property tax paid by a retail store is a cost of doing business. If that store is selling products in a very competitive market, the tax cannot be completely passed on in higher prices since the customers can switch to catalogue shopping or to stores that are more efficient. The tax thus results in lower profits to the owners. However, we should remember that owners include stockholders, and that most stockholders are also consumers. The pension plan to which you probably belong surely holds stocks, and lower profits reduce the investment income of that pension. Thus, even taxes not immediately shifted to customers or workers end up being paid by other consumers who happen to be direct or indirect business owners.

Borne by workers? Owners and stockholders are not the only ones who may be burdened with a tax that can't be shifted directly to customers. It also may be borne by those who work for the taxed business. For example, consider the unemployment insurance tax levied on business payrolls. This money goes to pay unemployment benefits to those who lose their jobs for reasons beyond their own control. While the business writes the check to the tax collector, it is likely that the cost of this tax is borne by the worker. A large employer who negotiates wages with its workers' union must consider not only the direct wages but also the related cost of fringe benefits and payroll taxes. If the employer is faced with higher payroll taxes, it may not be possible to pay the workers more. Thus, the tax on the business reduces the wages of the employee. It can work similarly in the case of smaller employers and nonunion workers.

Since the mid-1980s, Hawaii has increased taxes on the visitor industry, primarily by levying a hotel-room tax and by setting much higher property-tax rates on hotels and resorts than on residential properties. In each case, the tax burden probably is shifted, at least in part, to nonresidents. It is readily seen that the hotel-room tax probably will be shifted to "guests," mostly from out-of-state. In a different way, the higher tax on hotel property will reduce its value to the owners, but they probably will try to pass the tax on to hotel guests. If tourists react to the higher prices by vacationing elsewhere, hotels may lose some profits and hotel workers may lose some wages, or even jobs.

Who pays? Since tax shifting is an inevitable result of taxing businesses, it is important to understand the process and the consequences in order to make rational tax policy choices.

When indirect taxes are imposed on businesses, we don't know exactly who will bear them. Unlike an income tax paid by a readily identifiable household, the burden of an indirect tax is known only after the extent and direction of shifting have been measured. This is a difficult calculation since we don't know all the circumstances that will allow a business to shift or not shift its tax burdens. Yet, in spite of these difficulties, it is important to estimate shifting of indirect taxes. From a tax policy standpoint, it is critical that we have some idea who actually bears the burden of a particular tax. For example, an indirect business tax that is shifted to low-income consumers or workers may not be deemed desirable by policy makers.

Knowing to whom taxes are shifted provides some insight into the eventual burden of a business tax. Taxes largely shifted to consumers have a different impact than do taxes borne by business owners. For instance, a tax that cannot be shifted to consumers, workers or others will have a greater impact on high-income taxpayers since business owners tend to fall into that category.

A consultant retained by the Hawaii State Tax Review Commission studied the extent to which taxes were shifted in 1988. Of the $996 million collected in excise taxes, 90 percent was shifted to consumers, of which 63 percent was paid by Hawaii residents. Only 8 percent was actually borne by business owners, workers or suppliers. In contrast, of the $73 million in corporate income-tax collections, only 62 percent was shifted to consumers; 27 percent was borne by business owners.

The business-property tax is harder to trace. The commission study did not separate business and nonbusiness property taxes. However, in 1988 business accounted for 41 percent of all property tax collections.

Since the commission estimated that 52 percent of the property tax was paid by consumers, some business-property taxes had to be shifted to consumers.

Given that businesses "don't pay taxes" and the impact of indirect business taxes is so difficult to measure, why do we go through the effort to tax business?

Reasons for business taxes. There are both "good" and "bad" reasons for taxing businesses. One good reason is that it is easier for the government to collect sales or excise taxes from a few thousand businesses than from a million consumers. Another is that it may be the only way to "reach" out-of-state owners and consumers. Still another is that businesses (and thus their consumers, owners, workers and suppliers) benefit from such government services as roads, harbors, sewers, street lights and police protection, and should pay a share of their costs.

A bad reason for taxing businesses is the notion that businesses are better able to pay taxes than people are. This is nonsense. I hope that, by now, every reader understands that "businesses don't pay taxes, people do." Any attempt to increase business taxes will just place an additional strain on consumers, owners, workers, creditors or suppliers—people. When we tax business, we hide the true tax burden since the effects of shifting are neither easily measured nor well understood.

Hawaii's business taxes. Are business taxes in Hawaii "fair"? First, if business taxes are levied on the basis of the "good" reasons noted above, they can be considered fair.

Property taxes should reflect benefits received. Since, however, hotels, resorts, commercial and industrial property in Hawaii pay higher taxes than other property classifications, and it is doubtful whether business property benefits from government service more than other property, it would seem that the property tax is "unfair" in this way.

Another way to judge fairness is to see if our business taxes are out of line with those of other states. Hawaii's maximum corporate income tax is 6.4 percent. At least 30 states have rates above that. Hawaii's excise tax has a deceptively low 4 percent rate. Thirty states are above that. Thanks to our long-term high employment rate, unemployment taxes in Hawaii presently are lower than in virtually all other states. In 1988, only nine states had lower unemployment taxes.

Hawaii has been accused of being a "Tax Hell." Some of this is deserved, but most is not. In part, the reputation is not due to business taxes at all. Our individual income-tax rate (10 percent at its maximum) is one of the highest in the nation. Some of the reputation is due to nontax business costs. For example, Hawaii's regulatory environment, high land rents, high workers compensation insurance rates, high transportation fees and labor shortages all contribute to making it a costly place to live and conduct business. However, our business-tax rates are not out of line with those in other states. Taking into consideration all major business taxes, the State Tax Review Commission determined in 1984 that Hawaii's business tax burden was lighter than in most Western states, including California, Oregon and Arizona. This conclusion is dated, but nothing major has changed since then.

Thus, while some aspects of Hawaii's tax structure are burdensome to business, the overall tax environment is by no means "Hell." The reasons for that label will have to be found elsewhere in this book. My own picks include land-use policies that raise land prices and rents to exorbitant levels, the lack of competition in transportation and distribution, stifling regulatory policies, sky-high insurance costs and too few well-educated workers. All of these have greater impacts than the tax environment.

CHAPTER 21

COST OF HOUSING

SUMNER J. LA CROIX
Professor of Economics
University of Hawaii

"Can government make housing affordable?"

Between 1986 and 1990, housing prices in Honolulu soared to unbelievable heights. The median price of a single-family home in Honolulu rose from $159,700 to $345,000, and of a condominium apartment from $90,000 to $190,000. It became apparent to many low-income and middle-income families that they would never become homeowners as long as they lived in Honolulu. This incredible increase in housing prices across the entire range of the market provoked loud calls for state and city governments to take action. Predictably, politicians of all stripes responded by promising to provide more affordable housing.

Is it possible for new government policies to reduce housing prices in Honolulu? The answer is both "Yes" and "No." Yes—better government policies can accelerate housing development and reduce median prices. No—prices in Honolulu are likely to remain significantly higher than in most mainland cities regardless of the government's housing policies.

Primary reasons. Why aren't Las Vegas or even Seattle prices possible in Honolulu? Here are the primary reasons:

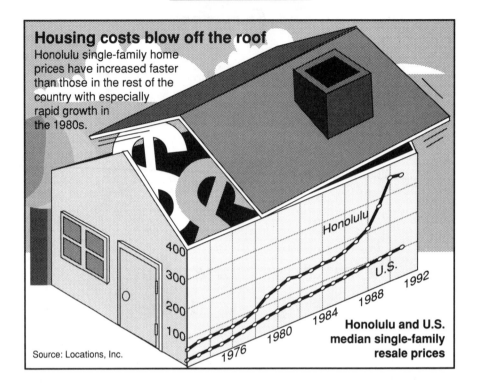

Housing costs blow off the roof
Honolulu single-family home prices have increased faster than those in the rest of the country with especially rapid growth in the 1980s.

Source: Locations, Inc.

Honolulu and U.S. median single-family resale prices

First, the obvious. Oahu is an island with a restricted amount of land onto which the city can expand. Much of its 380,000 acres is unusable for housing because of the island's two mountain ranges. The Pacific Ocean is, of course, the main barrier to Honolulu's expansion. University of Hawaii Professor Louis Rose compared housing prices in major U.S. cities and found that land scarcity is a major factor in skyrocketing housing prices. Out of 40 major U.S. cities studied, Honolulu has the least land potentially available for housing.

Second, housing prices are usually higher in cities where the quality of life is better. This is simply a reflection of supply and demand dynamics. Honolulu has many desirable qualities: clean air, clean water, warm winters and moderate summers, beautiful forests and mountains, spectacular views, a culturally diverse population, a wide spectrum of interesting restaurants and a varied night life. No place is right for everyone but, aside from the high cost of living, Hawaii is most people's idea of paradise. Even those (like me) who believe Honolulu's quality of life has slipped a bit over the past decade generally agree that it has slipped less here than elsewhere.

Third, the flow of tourists to Hawaii keeps increasing. The past decade was a period of spectacular growth for the tourism industry. Most experts believe that tourism will continue to grow, albeit at a slightly lower rate, as long as the islands' beautiful environment is conserved. If residents believe that future tourism growth will generate higher salaries for Hawaii's workers, then they will be willing to pay a higher price for a house or condo. They reason that their salaries will rise sufficiently to handle the debt burden. Of course, when individuals are willing to pay more, higher housing prices are no surprise. Again, we find simple supply and demand dynamics at work.

Fourth, Japanese investment has pushed up housing prices in Kahala, Waikiki, and nearby residential areas into which bought-out residents relocated. While the early 1990s slowdown in the Japanese economy could prompt some liquidation of investments, most experts anticipate that Japanese investors will continue to purchase homes in Honolulu. They predict that an increase in the number of investors from Hong Kong, Korea, Taiwan, Thailand and other countries will also push up Honolulu's housing prices.

Fifth, construction costs in Hawaii tend to be higher than on the Mainland. The reasons include: high shipping costs (largely because the federal Jones Act requires the use of expensive U.S.-built ships and crews between U.S. ports); high inventory costs (partly because of high land costs, but mostly because the distance from suppliers forces retailers to keep inventory levels extra high); Hawaii's relatively small population (which prevents certain economies of scale and, in many cases, results in a lack of competition); trade unions (which control the supply of construction workers); state licensing requirements (which restrict the entry of new contractors); excise taxes (which add about 5.5 percent to the cost of construction material); and, government exactions (such as the "60 percent-affordable-housing" and "one job for one new hotel room" programs). Most of these factors are beyond our control and the others are not likely to change soon.

Some forces pushing up prices could change at any time. Japanese investment could fall markedly; the clean, warm ocean waters off Waikiki could become polluted; workers' expectations of higher future incomes could change if other tourist destinations take off in popularity; and depletion of the ozone layer could conceivably make people leery of sun-drenched vacation spots.

Expectation and a ray of hope. My expectation is that housing prices here will remain much higher than on the Mainland as long as Honolulu retains its unique beauty, environment and cultural attractions. Mainland housing prices will only be attainable in the platforms of political parties.

Election year ballot box

There is, however, a ray of hope. A change in government housing policies could lead to lower housing prices, although not to mainland levels. To understand what these changes would be like, one must first understand the present situation.

The regulation of housing development in Honolulu is uniquely centralized. Most mainland urban areas are under numerous competing jurisdictions. The average has 72 governments. The New York City area has 360 and Chicago, 347. By contrast, Honolulu has just one local government. On the Mainland, if a single government in an urban area adopts a zoning policy that restricts housing development, prices change very little. Housing expands in another nearby jurisdiction with a less restrictive zoning policy. In Honolulu this can't happen. There are no other local jurisdictions.

Government monopoly. Not only does Honolulu have a monopoly on local government, but two agencies—the State Land Use Commission and the Honolulu City Council—have veto power over virtually any proposed development. If either agency dislikes a project, it's dead.

This structure has enabled government to pursue policies that have dramatically increased the cost of housing. First, only a small amount of island land has been zoned for urban use. The government has failed to approve numerous proposed housing projects and put fatal roadblocks in the way of other developments. Second, it has enacted regulations significantly increasing the cost of building new housing. For example, Honolulu's development plan, comprehensive zoning code, subdivision code, grading code and building code all impose heavy costs on developers. The existence of these rules and regulations means that developers must incur the cost of multiple studies, infrastructure to meet subdivision ordinances and project-design changes as mandated by government. In addition, the cost of resulting project delays—and there tend to be many—are considerable. Developers expect to take at least four to six years just to get the necessary approvals.

Why has government done this? Wouldn't approving more projects be politically popular? Defenders of the status quo argue that a heavy hand has been necessary to preserve Honolulu's pristine environment and relatively high quality of life. Certainly this is a partial explanation, but one that, frankly, rings hollow.

For a full explanation, one must consider who has benefitted. Besides reading Cooper and Daws' *Land and Power in Hawaii*, note that homeowners gain from high housing prices. Any policy action to reduce housing prices would impose capital losses on current owners. Since homeowners are more likely to vote in state and county elections, as well as to contribute money to politicians, don't look for more housing development tomorrow. Instead look for politicians to adopt band-aid programs, such as the 60 percent-affordable-housing requirement discussed in the Affordable Housing Requirement chapter. They may enable some middle-income families to become homeowners, but do nothing to expand the overall supply of housing.

In summary, high housing prices result from a number of factors, including unenlightened regulation that has helped current homeowners at the expense of everyone else. We can improve on our current institutions governing the housing market and achieve lower prices, but we should also beware of utopian proposals for mainland housing prices. Such proposals are good political rhetoric but are unattainable.

"WELL, THERE IT IS, AS PROMISED—
AFFORDABLE HOUSING."

THE HOUSING CRISIS

No issue before the Legislature today concerns more of Hawaii's people than that of housing.

The facts make dismal reading, so dismal perhaps that too many people in and out of government have too long ignored them:

- Prices for house sites in Hawaii are not only the highest in the nation, they have been reported as three times the national average.

- Not only do we have a shortage of low-income public housing, there are 36,000 Oahu families in the so-called "gap groups"— making too much to qualify for public housing but not earning enough to finance commercial mortgages . . .

- Home construction has fallen far behind need—10,000 units per year by one estimate . . .

The sum of all this is the word "crisis"—but as we have said before, the kind of crisis that has been so bad and with us so long we tend to forget it.

ONE OF THE FEW hopeful signs is that officials at the new State Capitol are aware and hopefully determined to do something about it . . .

The latest is the bipartisan proposal [that] . . . would establish a new State department of housing and urban affairs to run all State housing and land reform functions, along with starting important new programs to stimulate more and cheaper housing. . .

[The *Honolulu Advertiser*, March 23, 1969]

Highest rents

Apartment rents in Honolulu are the highest compared to other U.S. cities.

Location	Monthly rental costs	Index
Honolulu	$1,015	241.7
San Francisco	$772	183.7
Boston	$752	179.0
San Jose	$740	176.2
Washington, D.C.	$737	175.4
New York	$736	175.2
Los Angeles	$681	162.1
Chicago	$623	148.4
Hartford	$585	139.3
San Diego	$570	135.7
Standard City, USA	$420	100.0

The annual rental values shown in the above table are based on an 800-square-foot, 3-room, 1-bedroom, 1-bath rental unit. This accommodation is typical for a single renter earning $25,000 in annual income at Standard City, USA.

Source: Runzheimer International.

High rising rents

Honolulu apartment rents have increased faster than those in the rest of the country with especially rapid growth in the 1980s.

Source: Locations, Inc.

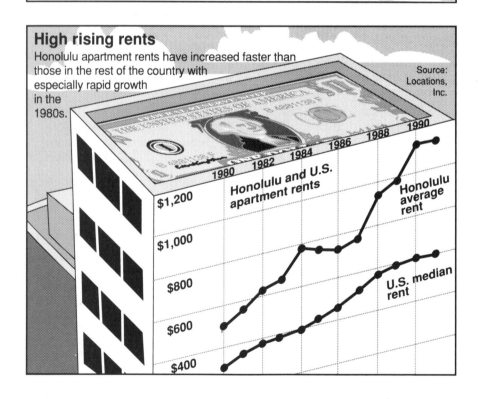

Honolulu and U.S. apartment rents

Honolulu average rent

U.S. median rent

$1,200
$1,000
$800
$600
$400

1980 1982 1984 1986 1988 1990

CHAPTER 22

HIGH RENTS

MICHAEL A. SKLARZ
Director of Research
Locations, Inc.

"Are rents in Hawaii high because of greedy landlords? Would rent control legislation help?"

Residential rents in Hawaii are high, when compared to the Mainland. The magnitude of the difference is shocking. This has been true for a long time and will be true for the foreseeable future. "Greedy landlords" occasionally have been blamed, and rent controls proposed, but the answer lies elsewhere.

From the perspective of rental property owners, rents in Hawaii are **low**! Think about it. A mainland investor usually can set rent at a level that will provide more than enough cash flow to cover debt service and operating expenses. Typically, mainland rents for a full year will be 8 to 10 percent of a property's value. In Hawaii, rents seldom are high enough to cover a new owner's cash flow needs, and usually amount to no more than 5 percent or so of the property's current value. Does that sound like "gouging"? Besides, if rents are so high, why don't "greedy landlords" build more rental properties in order to take even greater advantage of these "high rents"?

People (and entities) who own property in Hawaii are neither more nor less greedy than those in places where housing costs are low. With exceptions too rare to matter, property owners everywhere will sell or rent housing for the largest amount possible. It may be a sad commentary on human nature, but self-interest is the engine that powers our free-market economy.

Not enough housing. The high cost of housing can be traced to one disarmingly simple fact: for many years the supply of housing has lagged behind the demand. One result is that owners of existing rental housing units have enjoyed a "tight" market. For example, normal vacancy rates on the Mainland are about 1.5 percent for single-family homes and 6 to 7 percent for apartments. The vacancy rates in Hawaii have been less than a third of those, despite high rents! Plus, we cram ourselves into less space. Here in Hawaii, it is not uncommon for extended families to share housing. Even people who can afford to buy a newly constructed home generally have to make do with less space than would be acceptable elsewhere.

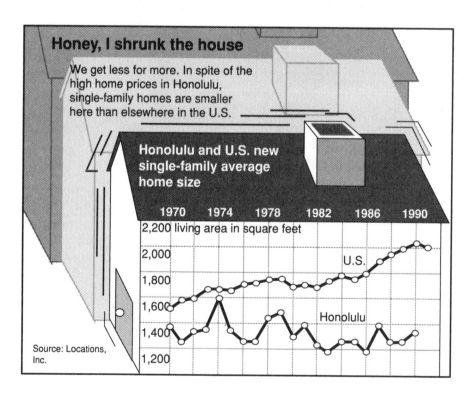

Honey, I shrunk the house

We get less for more. In spite of the high home prices in Honolulu, single-family homes are smaller here than elsewhere in the U.S.

Honolulu and U.S. new single-family average home size

Source: Locations, Inc.

The shortage of housing is not a deep, dark secret. You know it; I know it; government knows it. Our elected officials talk about this and try to give the impression that much is being done to correct the problem. You undoubtedly are interested in results. With that in mind, let's first take a peek at the bottom line. Oahu's housing inventory grew by 77,296 units during the 1970s, but by only 30,615 units during the 1980s. If every single-family unit currently (early 1992) planned for the 1990s actually gets built—and that's a big "if"—it will do no more than equal new demand. It will not even begin to eliminate what I estimate to be a current deficit of 15,000 housing units.

Government talks much about its success in providing "affordable housing." For the most part, these efforts have been focused on making home ownership possible for a very select group of people too poor to buy single-family homes at market prices and too rich to qualify for traditional forms of government assistance. Renters, however, probably realize that someone else's opportunity to buy a house for less than its market value (rather than at market value) does not address their problem of high rent.

Affordable rental housing has had to play second fiddle. Between 1982 and 1984, the Hawaii Housing Authority developed 373 housing units under the federal low-rent public-housing program. The number of new units dropped to 48 between 1985 and 1990, an average of less than ten per year. Is it any wonder that the waiting lists for public housing grew longer each year and homelessness increased? To be fair, the State's affordable housing initiatives involved a few low-rent projects, and officials are talking in 1992 about doing more. This is good, and should be encouraged, but in terms of numbers it may be too little, too late.

Government's direct involvement. We have in Hawaii a unique situation where state and county governments actually have gone into the housing development business, competing with the private developers they regulate. (This is as unfair to these developers as it would be for you to take your basketball team to the NCAA finals only to find the referee is the coach of the other team!) It's no surprise that many developers decided to shelve their plans.

The reason government housing agencies can build when private developers cannot is that only they have the advantages of insignificant

KAKAAKO
A PROJECT OF YOUR
STATE LEGISLATURE

land costs, the ability to borrow at municipal-bond interest rates, a virtual "free pass" in the lengthy regulatory process, and the luxury of not being required by shareholders to earn a profit.

Government, however, is not solely to blame for Hawaii's housing shortage. It is the work of an unlikely coalition of interests. This includes not only bureaucrats and elected officials who enjoy the perks of power, but also environmentalists who see development as destructive, anti-growth advocates who point out that reasonable housing costs will bring more people to Hawaii, and property owners who want their homes and investments at least to hold their values, and ideally to appreciate substantially.

Housing costs won't come down as long as this coalition successfully chokes off new development. Trust me, if the market were left alone (read that, if this cabal got out of the way), developers would trip over one another to take advantage of the strong demand for housing in Hawaii.

Rent control. Several public officials have suggested that rent control would be a great way to deal with high rents. The mechanics of rent control are simple: the government establishes and then maintains prices prevailing on a given date (say, as of today) on rental units. The intended beneficiaries are low-income families who are least able to afford rising rental prices of housing.

What are the results of rent control? Nothing at first. However, with the passage of time and as tenants' incomes rise, those living in controlled housing find they have more money to spend on nonhousing items. So far, so good.

However, the story continues and from here on out it is not a pleasant one. The housing shortage worsens as investors put their money elsewhere. And, despite laws intended to prevent it, controlled units often go to those who can best afford them. Potential tenants may be asked to pay extra ("key money") for the right to lease a place, and persons low on apartment waiting lists move up suddenly with appropriate payments to apartment managers. Families unable to pay such amounts increasingly are forced to crowd together because no new housing gets built.

Controlled housing often is allowed to deteriorate. The government can mandate minimum maintenance standards and even allow repair costs to be shifted to renters, but there is little incentive for landlords and it is hard to police. Los Angeles designed its rent control provisions with this problem in mind. But a 1991 study concluded that a counterproductive trade-off was unavoidable: "Efforts to reduce the costs of rent control, namely the deterioration and removal of dwellings from the rental stock, will generally be accomplished only by reducing the benefits received by tenants."

Another concern is that rent control can reduce the mobility of families. Moving from a controlled apartment generally requires that another be found, usually at an expense of time and money. This impacts most on the poor.

No easy answers. Don't get me wrong. The related problems of housing shortages and high rents are complex, and numerous judgment calls have to be made along the way. For example, if we do significantly increase the supply and get housing costs down, expect lots of newcomers. That may not seem so bad when unemployment is low, but it certainly will when unemployment is not so low.

If the cost of housing stays down and jobs stay plentiful, expect more traffic, more pollution and a noticeable reduction in the quality of life. Oh yes, and for all you homeowners and investors out there, don't be surprised if the inflation-adjusted value of your property falls.

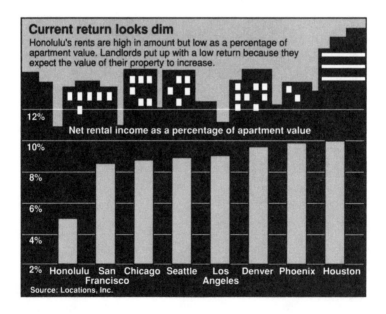

Current return looks dim
Honolulu's rents are high in amount but low as a percentage of apartment value. Landlords put up with a low return because they expect the value of their property to increase.

Net rental income as a percentage of apartment value

12% — 10% — 8% — 6% — 4% — 2%

Honolulu, San Francisco, Chicago, Seattle, Los Angeles, Denver, Phoenix, Houston

Source: Locations, Inc.

CHAPTER 23

SPECULATORS

LOUIS A. ROSE
Professor of Economics
University of Hawaii

"Is a tax on real estate speculators a good idea?"

One of the earliest accounts of speculation is found in the Old Testament. Joseph forecast seven years of feast for Egypt, to be followed by seven years of famine. He persuaded Pharaoh to acquire cheap grain in the flush years to be released later. Had this not been done, grain prices would have fallen through the floor during the crop-surplus years, and gone through the ceiling when crops failed. By stabilizing the grain market, Joseph and Pharaoh earned both profit and praise.

There is clear contrast between our positive attitude toward Joseph and Pharaoh, and prevailing negative attitudes toward today's speculators in land and housing.

Numerous antispeculation-tax bills were introduced at the State Legislature during the late 1980s and early 1990s, but none was enacted. Unquestionably, the issue will surface again.

Speculation defined. Several preliminary questions need to be answered before we can justify taxing speculators. To begin, what is speculation in real property?

Technically, anyone who buys a house is speculating, even if it's used as a principal residence, with no intention of a quick resale. For all home buyers hope that their purchase will be a good investment. But to most people speculation is buying nonpersonal-use property and trying to resell it as quickly as possible for as much as possible, without significantly improving it.

In a notorious 1990 case, a Honolulu property was bought for $166,000 and resold for $285,000—the same day! Obviously, the first buyer had no time to fix up the place or otherwise add to its intrinsic value. A quick profit of $119,000—not bad for a day's work.

Another highly publicized transaction involved five persons with very high city connections. Their *hui* made a $125,000 profit on a cash outlay of $5,000. The "market-priced" house they bought and sold on the same day was in a city-sponsored development. Observers grumbled more about influence peddling than about speculation, but no specific accusations were ever leveled, so I'll assume it was nothing more than another extreme example of speculation.

This kind of speculation (gigantic short-term profits) is simply a *symptom* of a troubled market. Nevertheless, in view of incidents such as these, it is easy to understand why many people think of speculation as *causing* the trouble by raising the price of housing in an unproductive and unfair manner.

Productive activities. Most speculation in real estate is accompanied by other activities that add substantial value. Developers (who, in a sense, are speculators) assemble land, make plans and get permits before construction can begin, and they put up or find the capital that makes new housing possible. All speculators produce useful information about the availability and value of property. This information sometimes leads to new construction and at other times to the sale of existing housing from one who values it less to another who values it more. Based on this, perhaps even the speculators described above did something productive!

In further defense of even extreme examples of speculation, quick resales do not establish value. Market value is determined by a large number of suppliers and demanders. Individuals cannot raise a house's value simply by wanting it to be more valuable. They can only search for potential buyers to whom the property has a higher value.

Can a large number of speculators raise home prices? Sure they can, but only for as long as they hold onto the housing. When they sell, the price tends to fall. Like their predecessors Joseph and Pharaoh, today's speculators do not raise the price permanently. Rather, they tend to even out fluctuations. In the long run, speculation actually reduces prices!

Are speculative profits fair? People concerned about the apparently unfair wealth distributive effects of speculation should think of the folks in the extreme examples provided above as lottery winners. (Again, I'm assuming only legal speculation was involved.) Their six-figure profits were far greater than the normal value of information and brokerage service provided, but "society" was not affected by these two-party transactions. Basically, it was a transfer of wealth from the original seller to the speculator.

But is it fair for the speculator to retain it all? To answer that we must first agree upon some rule of fairness. Suppose we accept the following productivity ethic: if profits are unearned because they result from community forces or government decisions or just plain luck, they should be taxed away and used to benefit the community. Under this fairness rule, profits could be kept only by those whose physical improvement of property causes the value to increase. The speculators I cited would be taxed on 100 percent of their gains.

Justifying a tax. Many people think it fair to tax speculators because they dislike opportunism or success based on luck. Others are envious of people whose wealth gives them the opportunity to speculate. To them a call for preventive or punitive measures seems only right.

There are two legitimate reasons for imposing any tax. One is to deter activities that we don't like. The other is to raise money to finance government. In many minds, these two reasons merge in the case of real estate speculation as surely as they do in alcohol and tobacco. Because they assume speculation is worse than just unproductive, that it *causes* permanently high prices, many people believe a special tax on real-estate profits would be just another "sin tax."

Tax on speculators could backfire. A substantial tax on speculative profits at a time when considerable housing is held by speculators surely would reduce the price of housing in the short run, and thereby temporarily make home ownership more accessible to first-time buyers. But it also would discourage increasing the supply of housing and this would lead to higher prices in the long run.

Approximately half of Honolulu's households are tenants.

Most of them are concerned about their monthly rents. A tax on speculation would have little effect on rents in the short run because speculators do not compete with tenants for actual use of housing. However, because the tax would discourage construction of new housing, after a few years the stock of rental units would dwindle and rents would rise.

It is impossible to design a tax that can effectively capture profits from real-estate traders without also adversely affecting developers, and (in the long run) both tenants and first-time home buyers. In all probability, the specific speculation tax bills considered by the legislature during the 1990, 1991 and 1992 sessions would have deterred development, construction and rehabilitation, as well as pure speculation. Besides, if someone wants to pay more for land or a house than it cost the current owner, why discourage the sale? A tax on speculative profits can do that.

Given all this, why do our modern Pharaohs even *propose* speculation taxes? It's because many are less interested in long-run solutions than in satisfying constituents to whom they are accountable at election time. And since elections occur frequently, short-run "gripes" get handled first. Thus, the long-run disadvantages of a speculation tax—a lower supply of housing with higher prices and higher rents— do not always receive much attention.

A few colleagues disagree. Several of my colleagues at the University of Hawaii agree with my analysis in the abstract, but not with my suggestion that it applies to Hawaii. They contend factors such as heavy-handed land regulation make our real estate market totally unique. They don't advocate a speculation tax, but neither do they believe such a tax would necessarily lead to less housing and higher prices. We have wonderful debates and are hopeful that this chapter will inspire equally lively discussions elsewhere.

"MAYBE THEY JUST WANT TO DISCOURAGE US FROM AFFORDABLE HOUSING..."

CHAPTER 24

AFFORDABLE HOUSING REQUIREMENT

BRUCE S. PLASCH
President
Decision Analysts Hawaii, Inc.

LOUIS A. ROSE
Professor of Economics
University of Hawaii

"Has Hawaii's affordable housing requirement been effective?"

For a lucky few, Hawaii's bold and innovative "affordable-housing" requirement has provided much-needed affordable homes. But the primary effect has been to *increase* housing prices and, as a result, to make most of the rich richer and most of the poor poorer. Furthermore, the requirement has decreased the availability of affordable homes in older neighborhoods and contributed to economic and social problems. Overall, the requirement has been a multibillion-dollar misjudgment.

Causes of high housing prices. Since before statehood, Oahu's housing prices have been among the highest in the nation. Major

THE PRICE OF PARADISE

factors which have contributed to high housing prices are: (1) the *strong demand for housing* resulting from a rapidly expanding economy driven primarily by the visitor industry; (2) the *finite supply of developable land* on a relatively small island having a mountainous interior; (3) *federal, state, and county* use of a large amount of developable land (for instance, military installations); (4) *restrictive government policies* designed to protect agricultural lands and environmentally sensitive areas, but which also restrict the supply of developable land (policies which have been partially relaxed in favor of developing homes on agricultural land in Ewa and in portions of Central Oahu); (5) the *very difficult, slow, and expensive approval process* which impedes the supply of land for housing, limits entry of new developers, and reduces competition among landowners and developers; (6) *insufficient construction of roads, water, sewers and other infrastructure* which further restricts the supply of developable land; (7) *high development fees* imposed on developers by government to cover the cost of infrastructure; (8) *high construction costs* due to shipping costs, high-markups necessitated by low volumes, high wages for construction workers, and other factors; and (9) *Japanese buyers* who, for a short period ending in 1990, added to the demand for luxury housing in a few East Honolulu neighborhoods.

An additional factor often cited as a cause of high housing prices is that the *ownership of land is dominated by a small number of owners* who can restrict the supply of developable land and thereby charge high prices for the land. Actually, however, major landowners have been willing to develop far more land than government has been willing to allow.

In spite of the presence of most of these conditions during the early 1980s, inflation-adjusted prices of single-family homes actually dropped from 1979 to 1986. Housing was becoming more affordable!

Affordable-housing requirement. In early 1988, when most major developers on Oahu were running out of land approved for residential development, the State—without public dialogue, legislative debate, or any analysis ever made public—imposed its new "60-percent-affordable-housing" requirement on major new subdivisions. The policy was hailed as a bold and innovative solution to Hawaii's housing crisis.

In justifying the requirement after the fact, the State argued that (1) the private housing market does not work properly since, without the requirement, developers build luxury homes rather than needed affordable housing (while new single-family homes in major subdivisions were indeed expensive prior to the affordable-housing requirement, most were typical tract homes priced about 20-percent **below** used single-family homes); (2) by granting approvals, government enables landowners and developers to realize enormous "windfall" profits, so it is fair for government to share in this windfall (in the form of the affordable-housing requirement which supposedly provides public benefits); (3) the loss of prime agricultural lands to housing requires that the public receive considerable benefits (i.e., affordable housing) in return; and (4) the allowed price of affordable housing is set so high that this is not a significant burden on developers.

On the surface, these justifications appear to have merit, and the affordable-housing requirement seems to offer a solution to Hawaii's high housing costs. Unfortunately, however, the affordable-housing requirement has contributed to housing becoming *less* affordable.

Restricted housing supply and higher prices. Before proceeding with a costly housing project, a developer must be satisfied that the project eventually will yield a reasonable profit. But under the 60-percent affordable-housing requirement, only 40 percent of the homes in the project—that is, the "market-priced" homes—must carry the burden of providing most or all of the profit. Consequently, some projects which would be profitable if all of the homes could be sold at market prices become unprofitable and are not initiated when only 40 percent can be sold at market prices. This is particularly true for projects having high development costs due to such factors as hillside locations, large development fees for interchanges, and high land and carrying costs.

The affordable-housing requirement has in fact affected development. In 1988, a major developer of typical tract homes calculated that a project would not be profitable under the affordable-housing requirement until prices of single-family homes increased by at least $20,000. Two other developers postponed indefinitely their submittals of subdivision applications because the requirement made their projects unprofitable. Yet another developer had problems securing financing for a project due to low profits caused by the requirement. Also, the number of subdivision applications submitted to the State decreased sharply in the early 1990s. Even government housing projects at that time encountered difficulties in meeting the requirement. Prices of their affordable units had to be increased because sales of "market" units would not generate the profits necessary to make the projects economically viable.

Because the affordable-housing requirement results in less housing being built, the supply of new housing is constrained. In turn, housing prices rise until demand is choked off sufficiently to bring demand in balance with the restricted supply. To varying degrees, the higher prices pervade the entire housing market, including rental and for-sale single-family homes, townhouses and condominiums. Of particular significance, the higher prices pervade the very large supply of *used* homes.

So what did happen after the affordable-housing requirement was implemented? Oahu's housing prices rose 90 percent in the three-year period ending in 1990, far surpassing price increases in major cities on the Mainland, including cities which experienced faster employment and population growth rates. Granted, additional factors were involved, including inadequate housing construction in the early 1980s due to extremely high interest rates, a lack of land approved for development, a strong demand for housing in the late 1980s due to the growth in the visitor and construction industries, higher development fees for infrastructure, and Japanese purchases of luxury homes in East Honolulu. Nevertheless, the affordable-housing requirement contributed to the rapid escalation in housing prices.

By 1992, it was generally recognized that the affordable-housing requirement was slowing the construction of new homes. In an effort to correct this situation, the State modified the requirement to allow developers greater flexibility in meeting it. However, the fundamental causes of high housing prices remained, including the negative effects of the modified affordable-housing requirement.

Economic and social effects. The affordable-housing requirement and the resulting increase in housing prices and rents has generated enormous impacts. A lucky few low- and moderate-income families have won housing lotteries (or were among the first in line) to buy homes at "affordable" prices which were significantly below-market prices. In effect, the wealth of these families increased.

Unfortunately, most low- and many moderate-income families have been hurt financially by the requirement. The renters and first-

"A STATE LOTTERY ABETS GAMBLING, GIVES PEOPLE FALSE HOPES, IS DEMEANING AND HARMFUL TO THE COMMUNITY..."

time home buyers who did not qualify for a housing lottery, or did not win one, have had to pay significantly more for their housing for the reasons discussed above.

Paradoxically, the primary beneficiaries of the affordable-housing requirement have been families who owned homes and rental property in 1987, before the requirement was imposed. Their wealth was increased substantially by the rise in housing prices which occurred in the late 1980s. The increase in wealth attributable to the affordable-housing requirement exceeded $2.4 billion for Oahu homeowners. (This estimate is based on approximately 120,000 single-family homes on Oahu in 1987, times the $20,000 increase in value discussed above for 1988, and excludes the increase in value of the larger number of condominiums.)

In effect, the affordable-housing requirement has made most of the rich richer and, except for a few lucky families, it has made most of the poor poorer.

The affordable-housing requirement and the resulting rise in housing prices has also reduced the supply of less-expensive homes in older neighborhoods by generating strong economic incentives to replace these perfectly livable homes with upscale homes. This is accomplished by renovating and enlarging older homes, or demolishing them to clear land for new, upscale homes. The developer thereby avoids the affordable-housing requirement as well as the infrastructure development fees required for new subdivisions. In the process, Oahu's supply of older less-expensive single-family homes in established neighborhoods diminishes.

The higher housing costs add to our economic and social problems. Renters and first-time home buyers who do not win a housing lottery have a lower standard of living; crowding is increased; many young people who cannot afford housing leave the islands; recruitment of teachers, professors, physicians and other professionals becomes difficult; attracting new businesses is inhibited, etc.

Solutions to high housing prices. The affordable-housing requirement demonstrates that, however well-intentioned, government intervention to dictate what should be produced and at what price can make a problem worse rather than better.

For homes to be priced within reach of moderate-income home

buyers and renters, it must be recognized that Hawaii is not exempt from the economic laws of supply and demand and the benefits of competition. This implies that government should attack aggressively the major causes of high housing prices listed above which slow development of new housing and inhibit competition among landowners and developers.

Although a larger supply of new homes and more competition among developers will allow future housing prices to be lower than would be the case under current policies, high housing prices will remain a problem for lower-income families. Well-focused programs to supplement incomes and provide other assistance to these families will still be required.

CHAPTER 25

GOLF COURSES

BRUCE S. PLASCH
President
Decision Analysts Hawaii, Inc.

"Should we allow so many golf courses to be built?"

Many residents believe that golf courses provide few benefits other than recreation for a small number of residents and rich tourists, take a lot of land and water that would be better used for farming or housing, require chemicals that pollute our environment, and drive up property taxes.

Contrary to these common perceptions, golf courses provide many benefits to Hawaii—benefits which far exceed those generated by many of Hawaii's other major users of land. Furthermore, with careful site and water-supply selection, and appropriate design and management, many golf courses can be built in Hawaii with minimal adverse impacts.

Demand for golf courses. As of early 1992, 68 golf courses operated in Hawaii, 14 more were under construction, another 13 had received major state and county approvals, and an estimated demand existed for another 23 by the year 2000—a potential total of 118 golf courses.

Benefits. The most obvious benefit of 118 golf courses is the recreation they will provide to about 17,000 golfers a day. Local golfers will be able to get tee times more easily (currently a major problem for golfers who are not members of private clubs), and green fees will be significantly lower than they would be if no new courses were built. Also, existing and new golf courses will provide about 21,000 acres of greenery scattered throughout the state, with the golfers paying the high cost of maintaining this greenery.

The primary economic benefit of *resort* golf courses is that they contribute to the economic health of Hawaii's largest industry and, in turn, to the economic health of the state. Golf courses help keep hotel rooms full of guests who tend to spend more than the average visitor and, as a group, are likely to visit Hawaii even during recessions. Because of golf's growing popularity, courses are regarded as virtual necessities for many resorts in order for them to remain competitive with other resort destinations around the world.

Also, the golf-course industry is a major employer in Hawaii and will soon provide more jobs than either the sugar or pineapple industries while using far less land. By the year 2000, golf courses are projected to provide 5,800 jobs using about 21,000 acres, compared with 5,360 jobs in sugar using nearly 162,000 acres in 1990, and 3,450 jobs in pineapple on nearly 31,000 acres.

Furthermore, by the year 2000, golf courses will provide about 2,300 grounds-maintenance jobs, compared with 3,080 and 1,850 field jobs respectively in the sugar and pineapple industries in 1990. Most of the grounds-maintenance jobs provided by golf courses are outdoor jobs involved with cultivating grasses and plants, applying fertilizers and chemicals, maintaining irrigation systems, etc. In terms of function, these jobs are similar to certain ones in agriculture, and require similar skills and training. These agricultural-type jobs are significant when one considers the declining agricultural employment in Hawaii and the number of new graduates in agriculture who need jobs.

Many golf courses also serve as cost-effective drainage channels and flood-retention basins. As such, they are far better solutions to drainage and potential flooding problems than are concrete-lined storm drains, in that golf courses are far more attractive, the grasses filter out silt and nutrients thereby reducing pollution of coastal waters, and the retained rainwater seeps into the ground to restore the groundwater supply.

In a number of cases, golf courses serve as buffers and safety zones to protect residents from nuisance activities.

Comparative benefits. If the sugar industry (our dominant land user) is considered to be good for Hawaii—and most people do believe this—then golf courses should be regarded as better, since they provide far more benefits and impact the environment far less (see Table 1). Compared to 180 acres in sugarcane (which is a tall grass), a golf course provides greater recreational opportunities and access, far more jobs, more agricultural-type jobs, more high-level jobs, greater employment security, far higher tax revenues, lower water consumption, less demand on potable water sources, a less disruptive impact on land, a cleaner environment, and a more favorable impact on neighboring properties. Similar comparisons apply to most other types of agriculture.

This is not to suggest that golf courses should replace agriculture. Actually, it is possible to have both.

Compatibility with agriculture and housing. Assuming that the estimated demand for golf courses to the year 2000 is to be met, then an additional 23 golf courses must be approved. The land required would amount to about 4,100 acres, about one-third the acreage of an average sugar plantation. This land requirement can be met easily without adversely affecting existing agricultural activities or the growth of diversified agriculture, using (1) less than 0.5 percent of the more than one million acres of "junk" lands in the State Agricultural District that are *unsuitable* for commercial crops due to poor soils or expensive water (lava lands in West Hawaii, for example); or (2) less than 4 percent of the 120,000 acres of land which, since the late 1960s, has already been released from plantation agriculture; or (3) some combination of the two.

Similarly, new golf courses need not take up land that could otherwise be used for housing. In developing urban areas, locations suitable for golf courses but not housing include drainage ways that are subject to occasional flooding, areas within potential blast zones surrounding munitions depots, high-noise zones near airports or under flight paths, land under high-voltage lines, and areas having soils that would be unstable for housing foundations. Most of the new and planned golf courses in Ewa and central Oahu fall into one or more of these categories.

Water requirements. Water for golf courses can be a more difficult issue than land. Nevertheless, water sources are available that would not adversely affect the availability of water for domestic or agricultural use. These include brackish water (too saline for domestic consumption or most farming, but not for salt-tolerant golf-course vegetation); treated wastewater; areas where the supply is abundant due to heavy rainfall or cutbacks in sugar and the supply far exceeds potential demand; and water that is not desired by other users, possibly because it would be too expensive to deliver for agricultural or urban use.

To a significant degree, golf courses can help solve water-supply problems. When treated wastewater is used for irrigation, a portion seeps down to recharge the groundwater supply and becomes available for reuse to irrigate other greenery. In the process, the wastewater is stripped of nutrients and contaminants by the filtering action of the grass and soil. Thus, the water is recycled rather than being lost when it is pumped into the ocean.

Environmental impacts. A concern often raised about golf courses is that the fertilizers and chemicals used on them will run off and may contaminate groundwater supplies or pollute streams and coastal waters. Although golf courses are inappropriate for environmentally sensitive areas such as wetlands, extensive monitoring of the environmental impacts of golf courses in Hawaii has led university researchers to conclude that they rarely cause environmental problems, and that they are one of the most benign human uses of land. On a professionally managed golf course, problems are spot-treated, resulting in much less impact than occurs with most agricultural and urban activities.

Property values and taxes. Farmers and residents have expressed fear that if a golf course is built in their neighborhood, then property values and taxes will rise. However, the increased land values are generally limited to lots that *front* the courses, with most of the increase in value being captured by the project developers. Furthermore, property taxes will not change for lands dedicated to agriculture, since the tax is based on the low agricultural value of the land, rather than on its much higher market value.

For homeowners whose property values do rise, the associated increase in property taxes is comparatively small. For example, for Oahu homeowners, each $1,000-increase in the value of a lot (and the resulting increase in the wealth of the homeowner) results in an increase in property taxes of only 27 cents a month (1991/92 rates).

In summary, with proper site selection and management, golf courses provide far more benefits with far fewer adverse impacts than are generally recognized.

Table 1
GOLF COURSE VS. SUGAR OPERATIONS:
COMPARATIVE BENEFITS AND IMPACTS (180 acres)

Item	Golf Course	Sugarcane
Recreational Opportunities and Access	100 to 300 golfers a day	None
Employment: Total jobs Agricultural-type jobs High-level jobs Employment security	30 to 80+ 15 to 22 5 to 14 Stable	About 6 3.3 1.7 At risk
Tax Revenues: State tax revenues: -Construction-related -Operations (excise tax on final sales) County tax revenues (property taxes)	Up to $14 mil. (net) Up to $200,000 a year (net) Up to $240,000 a year (net)	Not applicable None About $1,000 a year
Water: Use Quality	About 0.7 mgd Brackish or treated effluent	About 1.5 mgd Sweet to slightly brackish
Impact on Land	Major features preserved	Major features altered
Environmental Impacts: Construction or harvesting and planting Operations	Soil runoff (one-time) Small risk of chemical runoff and leaching	Greater soil runoff, dust, noise & smoke More chemicals, rodents
Impact on Neighboring Properties	Enhanced	Degraded

CHAPTER 26

DEVELOPMENT FEES

David L. Callies
Professor of Law
William S. Richardson School of Law
University of Hawaii

"Why would anyone oppose the $100 million golf-course development fee proposed by Mayor Fasi?"

Why not $200 million? or $300 million? As a U.S. Senator declared back in the '50s, "A hundred million here, a hundred million there, pretty soon you're talking about real money"! The money would be used for affordable housing. With thousands of folks willing to line up days in advance for a few hundred subsidized housing opportunities, who in Hawaii can quarrel with the need? But is arbitrarily whacking golf-course developers going about solving the housing crisis the right way?

It is only natural to applaud any effort to shift some of the cost of government to people who seemingly can better afford it—in this case to golf-course developers and golfers willing to pay exorbitant club dues and green fees. But laws (such as the U.S. Constitution) designed to protect us from the tyranny of the majority should not be ignored, even when the aggrieved parties are either hesitant to assert their own rights or perceived as well-heeled foreigners.

The proposed $100 million impact fee is arbitrary in a variety of ways. The amount itself had to have been pulled out of a hat. Evidently the mayor believes developers are willing and able to pay. This may have been true when the fee was first proposed, but the market in Japan for memberships in such courses plummeted in the early 1990s. And make no mistake, that's the only market that ever could have supported such a price tag.

Maybe after the demand for golf-course permits softens, other items will be put on sale: $25 million for tennis courts? $10 million for a bowling alley? And why stop with sport facilities? Maybe permits for university branches can be sold at auction.

All of this—including the $100 million golf-course impact fee—is pure silliness.

Proper use of fees. Impact fees are supposed to be charges on land development that compensate government for related costs. Through them, developers pay for new (or better) roads, water, sewers, parks, schools, open spaces, libraries, police and fire stations, sanitary landfills and, yes, in some jurisdictions, low-income housing—but only if their need can be rationally tied to a particular land development. In this sense, the development impact fee is a necessary and a proper use of governmental power.

Clearly, golf courses should pay their way. The cost of public facilities needed because of them should be borne by the developer.

How much capital facility cost can we stick on golf courses? Not very much. Golf courses will certainly increase traffic, so a road impact fee is rational. They also need water, and they need to dispose of waste-water and refuse. Therefore, water, sewer and landfill fees also would be reasonable. This could total $10 million or so. But how in the world does a golf course generate a need for housing? Some folks like to live around a golf course, but they aren't the ones in need of affordable housing.

The right to use one's own property as he or she sees fit (except when it is somehow harmful to neighbors or the public at large) is guaranteed by the U.S. Constitution. Golf courses tend to be good neighbors.

The State and the counties are responsible for the regulation of land use. Selling zoning permits for what the market will bear is not regulation. Indeed, it is impossible to charge "top dollar" for permits while properly regulating land use. For example, any developer paying $100 million is likely to insist upon a "choice" location, even if it is not ideal from the community standpoint.

Legitimate approaches. There may be legitimate ways to make golf-course developers pay extra. The first is for county governments to be more systematic in calculating development fees. The Hawaii State Tax Review Commission has pointed out that the counties generally have done a poor job of making these calculations. In fact, amounts often have been *ad hoc* determinations, typically too low to cover the full impact of development. This not only shortchanges the people of Hawaii but also makes it impossible to determine whether favors were involved. The public trust demands that the process of calculating development fees be aboveboard and based upon clear guidelines.

A second legitimate approach is a development tax (rather than a fee). The State could levy this or could give counties authority to do so. A shift of taxing authority from the State to the counties is as likely as my chances of winning next year's Hawaiian Open. But a state tax on golf-course development is not all that farfetched. The State so far has not enacted such a tax primarily because there is no compelling reason for it. After all, why should golf courses be discouraged or otherwise treated separately? And, unlike development fees, a tax would have to be according to a preset objective formula. There would be no room for subjectivity and so a measure of power would be lost.

A third possible legitimate approach is through converting the use of land from a "right" to a "privilege." In order to establish a privilege approach, however, it would first have to be agreed that government actions, such as zoning decisions, create and destroy land value. This is the "windfalls/wipeout" theory. Its bottom line is that since government grants the privilege of development, it can charge whatever it likes for the privilege. However, to be consistent and fair, when government destroys value, it must compensate the landowner for that destruction as well.

That's the way it worked in England for about half of the twentieth century. First the government wiped out property owners by nationalizing development rights, then required permission for *any* development, with a whopping (as much as 100 percent) "windfall" charge.

This approach may not be attractive for several reasons. First, paying for a development-rights "wipeout" in Hawaii would be astronomically expensive. Second, private land development likely would slow dramatically as the cost of major projects approached nonprofitability. When land development premiums get too high—like maybe $100 million per golf course—private development stops completely.

An arbitrarily set $100 million premium on golf courses would violate constitutional rights and be a just plain bad idea. Let's get government back to doing its job—keeping development out of areas where it is harmful, and charging for a fair share of the public costs involved. Low-income housing and other general problems of society are the responsibility of all taxpayers. If developers want something a little extra from government, let them bargain for it through a development agreement.

"THERE'S AN ALTERNATIVE TO AFFORDABLE HOUSING: AFFORDABLE DONATION TO THE STATE FUND..."

CHAPTER 27

WATER POLICY

JAMES E.T. MONCUR
Professor of Economics
University of Hawaii

"Why is government allowing new development and golf courses when water is so scarce that we have to ask for it in restaurants?"

Anyone who has lived in Honolulu more than a few weeks has encountered Board of Water Supply (BWS) trucks with the slogan "Pure Water—Man's Greatest Need." Yet the Board wants us to abandon the time-honored expectation of a glass of water in a restaurant.

A friend of mine claims every faucet in New York City leaks. An exaggeration, of course, but how is it that uptight New Yorkers can be so careless about their plumbing while we in Honolulu now have to ask for a glass of water? One would think water is not scarce at all in New York, while in semitropical Hawaii water is rare and dwindling. This impression is probably wrong in both places.

No one doubts that we all need water but Honoluluans and New Yorkers alike must ask two questions: How much water do we really need? Under what legal and institutional conditions do we get it?

Water departments in both Honolulu and New York City—and many in between—fret increasingly about their inability to satisfy growing water demand in the manner to which we users have become accustomed. Traditionally, as populations grew and economic activities required more water, the water agencies would simply go out and find new sources—"supply augmentation." But new sources have become more and more difficult and costly to come by. "Demand management"—inducing conservation—is the other possibility.

For either supply augmentation or demand management to succeed, the price we pay for water and the legal and institutional conditions of our water use must be set right. With the right pricing and suitable property rights, we would find that water is not really scarce in Honolulu, at least not in any degree to cause serious concern.

Water Pricing. A higher price would convince many of us that our water "needs" are less intense and inflexible than we thought. Hosing down the driveway, watering lawns, and even bathing, housecleaning, laundry and cooking habits can be adjusted. Any number of studies, for Honolulu as well as other places in the world, confirm this responsiveness to higher water rates.

The price New Yorkers pay (or rather the price they don't pay) is an important reason for their lackadaisical attitude toward wasted water. New York City has traditionally covered the costs of its water department by levying a flat fee on all customers. In return, people can use as much water as they want. The New York City water department has no way of knowing how much water individual customers are using—very few of the city's dwellings and businesses have meters. Without metering, the water department cannot bill customers in proportion to their use. People thus have no personal incentive to worry about wastefulness. The only "cost" of letting the faucet leak is the sound of dripping water.

Like New Yorkers, Honolulu apartment dwellers generally lack a personal price incentive for conserving water. Most apartment and townhouse projects are "master metered," with one bill for the entire complex sent to the owner or owners' association. Single-family dwellings and business structures, on the other hand, pay (as of 1992) $1.34

per thousand gallons, plus a billing fee.

Most agricultural use on Oahu, including sugar and pineapple, is self-supplied. The BWS has relatively few agricultural customers, who together account for only 2 or 3 percent of total water delivered. These few, however, have been a potent political force, as indicated by a preferential rate structure. After buying the first 13,000 gallons at the same rate as everyone else, they pay only $0.69 per thousand gallons. That price is no great incentive to conserve.

The BWS's charter requires that it cover its costs. To do so, it has had to raise water rates considerably in the past few years. Even so, a number of real, but non-cash costs are ignored. For example, the Board does not count as "cost"—at least not for rate-making purposes—the accumulation of mains, pumps and other equipment contributed by developers over the years. The BWS eventually will have to replace this infrastructure and so it really should take it into account in calculating costs. Also, it should recognize that inflation alone will boost replacement costs to several times the original. Finally, if water scarcity is truly increasing, like oil it has value just sitting in the ground. Currently, the BWS ignores this scarcity value. All things considered, the true economic cost of water is substantially higher than the amount we now pay. In fact, the current price, adjusted for inflation, is not much more than it was 20 years ago.

Honolulu does not differentiate between high and low cost customers. Homesites at high elevations, for example, require much pumping to bring water up from wells close to sea level. Despite the high cost of this pumping, hilltop customers pay the same $1.34 per 1,000 gallons as everyone else. Until recent rate hikes, the BWS's cost of pumping water to the top of some posh neighborhoods in Honolulu probably exceeded what these generally well-off customers paid for it.

Finally, the BWS is a government agency, albeit a semi-autonomous one. By charter, its revenues cannot exceed its costs. Managers and staff cannot benefit from raising rates and, given their engineering backgrounds, their orientation is toward augmenting the supply. The thought of clearing the market by means of raising prices, instead of finding new water sources, may not have even occurred to them. Certainly, that approach would devalue their engineering degrees and experience.

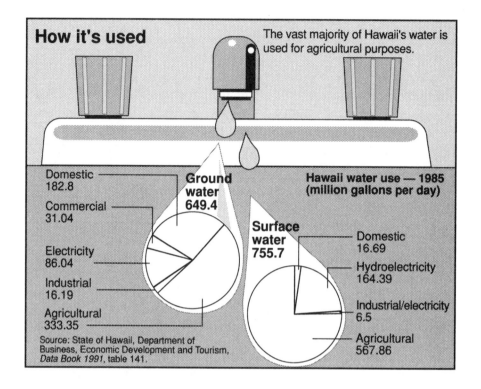

How it's used

The vast majority of Hawaii's water is used for agricultural purposes.

Domestic 182.8
Commercial 31.04
Electricity 86.04
Industrial 16.19
Agricultural 333.35

Ground water 649.4

Surface water 755.7

Hawaii water use — 1985 (million gallons per day)

Domestic 16.69
Hydroelectricity 164.39
Industrial/electricity 6.5
Agricultural 567.86

Source: State of Hawaii, Department of Business, Economic Development and Tourism, *Data Book 1991*, table 141.

As a monopoly, the BWS has no competitive pressure. Raising rates results in complaining customers in the short run, regardless of the long-run benefits. All told, the incentive is to keep rates as low as possible consistent with good service—whatever the true economic cost.

As of 1988, the most recent year for which figures are available, Oahu's two sugar plantations accounted for 44 percent of the 408 million gallons used on the island in an average day. Much of this water is well-positioned to serve new urban areas and could conceivably be transferred to supplement stretched-thin urban sources. What are the prospects for such transfers?

Legal and institutional framework. I began by chiding New York. For equal-opportunity bashing, let's turn to California. West Coast water waste comes not so much from lack of metering as from lack of a well-defined property right in the water. Farmers can get water (from federal Bureau of Reclamation projects) that generally can't be sold to nonfarmers. Federal water projects were intended to help farmers, not cities; no necessity or procedure for transferring the water out of agriculture was ever envisioned. Thus, California farmers continue to irrigate low-value crops such as cotton and alfalfa. Even with cheap federal water, these crops often depend on government price supports for continued viability.

California farmers pay very little for this water. Their rates are determined mainly by project construction outlays many years and much inflation ago, and often heavily subsidized from the beginning. More than one researcher has pointed out the absurdity of Southern California communities' having to pay in excess of $1.50 a thousand gallons for new water (plus the cost of transporting it) while irrigators commonly pay only a tenth or twentieth of that to grow crops in surplus nationally. And yet that's exactly what's happening.

Like California, Hawaii has many acres of land in agriculture, particularly sugar. Sugar plantations, or the landowners (not necessarily the same people), are obvious potential sellers of water. Like some of California's crops, sugar production probably would not survive without federal support. Unlike California, however, water for Hawaii sugar was developed privately, with no federal subsidies. Much of it was done before statehood and under a water-rights regime that by the 1970s had evolved into a highly flexible, efficient, market-oriented system. Irrigators felt an ownership in water rights, which they frequently bought and sold as their uses changed. Because the right to sell as well as the right to use were clearly defined and unquestioned; those who had "surplus" water—which they valued lower than someone else was willing to pay for it—had every incentive to quit whatever they were doing with it, and sell it to the willing buyer. That, of course, worked to everyone's advantage—a classic win-win result.

But a 1973 court decision, a 1978 amendment to the State Constitution and the 1987 State Water Code have combined to stop such transfers. The Hawaii Supreme Court declared in 1973 that the State, not individuals or companies, was in some sense the owner of the water. This reversed more than a century of practice and law on the subject. The 1978 constitutional amendment was an attempt to solidify the control offered by that decision. The water code failed to define what

is meant by a water right, raised uncertainty on the question of transferability of such rights, and erected a state bureaucracy with broad powers to approve or disapprove water transfers.

Causes of "shortage." These three developments have combined to create one gigantic mess. The prospect for orderly water transfers is dim; the prospect for conflict in the use of water grows daily. This lose-lose situation bears much of the responsibility for the resulting water "shortage."

On the supply side, imminent shortages stem as much from these institutional barriers to transfer as from physical limitations. On the demand side, the poorly calculated and inversely structured BWS water rates lead to overuse. Government activity is at the core of both these problems.

I hope this all sounds crazy to you—because it is. Do our political leaders think they are "solving" the water shortage by prohibiting restaurants serving water except on request? They might as well ask us to empty the ocean with teaspoons. Some say this new rule sensitizes everyone to the need to conserve water. But the rule mostly just distracts people from the real cause of the "shortage," and paves the way for supply augmentation and the higher costs that have been and will continue to be a natural consequence of Hawaii's unenlightened water policy.

CHAPTER 28

BALLOT-BOX ZONING

DAVID L. CALLIES
Professor of Law
William S. Richardson School of Law
University of Hawaii

"Why shouldn't we be able to vote on land-use decisions?"

Many people—especially those pleased when the initiative was used to stop development in 1990 near Sandy Beach—believe that the public should indeed be allowed to vote on land-use decisions. I don't.

We live in a representative democracy, not the simple kind where everything is subject to popular vote. We elect governors to execute the laws and representatives to make legislative decisions, and to appoint judges and administrators to interpret and administer the laws. We have agreed to limit our own constitutional right to vote for a simple yet compelling reason: we as individual citizens simply don't have the time, expertise or energy necessary to micromanage the day-to-day affairs of government.

Our county charters provide us with limited power to require certain laws (the initiative) and to review others adopted by our representatives (the referendum). We do this by petitioning to put something on the ballot at the next general election. Thousands of signatures are required. If enough people vote "Yes" at the general election, it becomes law. This form of direct democracy has much to be said in its favor.

Terrible idea. But using the initiative or referendum to make land-use decisions—"ballot-box zoning"—is a terrible idea for lots of good reasons.

First, it's illegal. Our State Supreme Court said so in 1989. Of course, this reason could be eliminated by simply changing the law, and that's why supporters of ballot-box zoning are familiar faces at the legislature.

Second, a lot of careful planning should go into land-use decisions. Ballot-box zoning upsets the planning process. Before a county can rezone property, it must see what the county general and development plans *and* the state plan and 12 functional plans have to say about it. If we can vote to rezone a neighbor's land at a general election, the entire planning process goes out the window.

Third, ballot-box zoning lets a majority of voters decide how someone else's land is used. Why should they be able to do that? A neighbor's use of his or her land is generally none of their business. It is not, as the courts describe it, a legislative decision. Rather, it's a decision which affects the owner most, and maybe others who live close by. The courts call this an administrative or quasi-judicial decision.

If we can all vote on decisions affecting the use of specific parcels of land, why shouldn't we be able to overturn other judicial and quasi-judicial decisions, like speeding tickets or child custody? Would you like your neighbors to be able to vote up or down on things like that?

True, some states have decided that a specific rezoning was a legislative act even though it seemed to affect only the owner of the property. In those situations, people were allowed to vote on rezoning at general elections. Their state constitutions specifically provided for initiative and referendum. Ours in Hawaii does not. Of course, it could. We could amend our State Constitution and then our courts *might* permit ballot-box zoning. I say might because, even in states with initiative and referendum in their constitutions, some courts have decided that zoning is too personal to the landowner to permit the public to decide.

What would happen. What happens if we do amend our constitution and our courts say ballot-box zoning is OK? Several things, none of them very good. First, the land development process becomes even more complicated than it already is. After spending years obtaining state and county land reclassifications and approvals, the landowner may then have to roll the dice on a countywide election. If the landowner loses, everything will have been in vain. The only recourse is to file a lawsuit asserting that the initiative or referendum was arbitrary and unreasonable, or that the zoning change was a "taking." Both are hard to do, and require a lot more time and money.

The island of Kauai learned first-hand how developers react to such possibilities. The Graham Beach Partnership (GBP) spent years getting its Nukolii hotel and condo resort development through the state and county planning processes. After it had what it thought were all necessary approvals and permits, and was midway into the construction of the first of two buildings, the people of Kauai in a referendum nixed the whole project. GBP then spent a great deal of money on attorney fees only to have the Hawaii Supreme Court declare that once a referendum petition has been properly filed, the referendum becomes yet another hurdle to be cleared before development can safely begin. A great victory for the people of Kauai, right?

Not quite. Understandably, GBP and other developers did not like the possibility of totally unexpected and unpredictable last hurdles. The time and expense involved in getting that far into the process was too great. So they focused on development elsewhere.

At first, the people of Kauai who had supported the referendum were delighted. No growth meant their beloved island would not be spoiled. Then Hurricane Iwa in November of 1982 devastated Kauai's tourist industry and people began to appreciate the indirect benefits of tourism, previously taken for granted. People with jobs seemingly unrelated to tourism found their futures darkened. The value of a pristine environment dropped in the face of widespread unemployment.

Kauaians in 1984 voted a second time on the Nukolii project, this time reinstating the original approval. Soon development activities were above pre-referendum levels. Kauai learned the hard way the consequences of using the referendum to derail just one project. Hopefully, Oahu and the other islands learned something from afar.

A practical reason. Perhaps the most important practical reason ballot-box zoning is a terrible idea is that the voting booth is not the

"WITH SUCH SHOW OF OVERWHELMING SUPPORT FROM LEGISLATORS...HOW'D IT DIE?..."

best place to address complicated zoning issues. In California, where initiatives and referendums are common, voters receive election "books" describing each proposition to be decided in the next election. These books regularly exceed a hundred pages each from the state and local governments. Most citizens lack the time, energy or expertise to plow through complicated technical material before voting. As a result, a special-interest group with the slickest advertising campaign often decides which ballot propositions get passed and which do not. Neither side may address the specifics; advertisements proliferate with nothing more than "vote YES on number 21"!

Do we want this in Hawaii? After all, it is not as if permission to rezone and develop land in Hawaii is given secretly or without public participation. All rezoning requires several public hearings before one of our four county councils, and at least one before a planning commission. Citizens routinely testify before both. Furthermore, most land development—particularly if it is near the shoreline—requires some other kind of permit regardless of the zoning. This also requires a public hearing at which voters can testify. Often, state agency hearings are required as well. In short, we have plenty of public hearings and public participation.

What we do not have is ballot-box zoning. And for all the foregoing reasons, we shouldn't.

CHAPTER 29

LEASEHOLD CONVERSION

JAMES MAK
Professor of Economics
University of Hawaii

"Why would government force landowners to sell their land to lessees?

Hawaii is unusual in that a large percentage of its housing is on leasehold land. The homeowner owns the house but not the land. Most of this leasehold residential housing is in Honolulu.

Residential leasehold wasn't a major factor in Hawaii's housing market until after World War II. During the early 1960s, nearly seven out of every ten new single-family houses were built on leasehold land. By 1975 some 30,543 owner-occupied units in Honolulu were on leased land; 85,265 were on fee-simple land.

In other countries—such as Israel and Singapore—where residential land leasing is common, the government typically is the landowner and usually the land rents are artificially low. In contrast, nearly all lessors in Hawaii are private parties. When leasehold was at its peak, the Bishop Estate, the largest private landowner in the state, had most of the residential leases, followed by the Castle Foundation, the Castle Estate and the

Campbell Estate. Absent legal restraints, nongovernmental landowners generally will charge market land rents.

For a variety of reasons, these landowners opted to lease rather than to sell their land. In the case of the Bishop Estate, a major factor was that the trustees feared the loss of the estate's tax-exempt status and the ensuing requirement to pay federal and state capital-gain taxes.

Once attractive. In the 1950s, 1960s and early 1970s, if a fee-simple home wasn't available, buying a leasehold home didn't seem too bad a deal. Because houses built on leasehold land cost less than identical ones on fee-simple land, home buyers could either make a smaller down payment or, for the same price, buy a larger home. The typical 55-year lease with rents fixed for the first 30 years at affordable levels didn't seem unreasonable. For example, the land rent on a typical home in Kamiloiki Valley in Hawaii Kai was fixed at less than $13 a month for the first 30 years.

Why were land rents so low? The simple answer is that when lease rents were first set no one—landowners or lessees—imagined how land values would appreciate in Honolulu.

It all seemed too good to be true to the lessees, and it was! Lease rents eventually had to be renegotiated. Despite a state law passed in 1975 to regulate how much ground rents could be increased, the new rents were more than ten times the old rents. Lessees who acquired their leasehold homes nearly 30 years earlier suddenly faced huge jumps in payments at a time when many contemplated retirement and lower incomes. All of a sudden, leasehold housing didn't seem so attractive.

Paying market rent is a bit like buying the land outright on an installment plan, except that when you buy the land, the mortgage interest is tax deductible. Lease rents are not tax deductible. This makes leasehold housing more expensive than fee-simple housing. Also, installment notes eventually get paid off, whereas lease payments not only never go away, they continue to increase periodically.

Some lessees who can't afford to pay the ever-increasing rent indefinitely are forced to sell their homes, but at a reduced price due to the higher lease rent. Frustrated by the situation, lessees banded together to demand that government force the lessors to sell them the land outright. Most landowners wanted no part of this. Some simply did not want to sell. Others said they didn't mind selling, but doubted that judges and juries would set a fair sales price.

Who gets the appreciation? In a nutshell, the resulting (ongoing) struggle between landowners and lessees is over who gets the lion's share of 30 years of appreciation in land values. One Bishop Estate trustee accused the lessees of trying to steal Bishop Estate's land. Lessees, of course, see it differently.

In 1967 the State Legislature passed a law allowing the State to condemn residential land under single family homes and then sell it outright to the lessee owner-occupants. The constitutionality of this landmark legislation was upheld by the U.S. Supreme Court in 1984 and the Hawaii Supreme Court in 1985. Since then, nearly 14,000 leasehold single-family residential lots have been converted to fee simple, either through direct negotiation between landowners and lessees or through condemnation proceedings. As of 1992, only 4,600 leasehold single-family residential lots remained in Honolulu. Moreover, since the passage of this law, no new leasehold single-family residential tracts have been developed in Honolulu. Although the U.S. Constitution requires sellers to be compensated justly when properties are condemned, the Bishop Estate and other landowners insist that these forced sales have not resulted in fair compensation to them. Lessees argue just the opposite. Thus far, no one has established conclusively that the compensation has been anything but "fair."

Land reform. This so-called "land reform" law applied only to owner-occupants of leasehold single-family houses. Leasehold condominium and co-op apartments and townhouses were not included. In 1991, the Honolulu City Council passed a measure patterned after the State's land-reform law, thus enabling over 20,000 owner-occupants of multi-family leasehold dwellings to buy the fee interest under their homes. Bishop Estate has challenged the legality of this measure.

Why have both the State of Hawaii and the City and County of Honolulu taken the side of the lessees? After all, weren't all those lease contracts voluntarily signed years ago? Didn't all subsequent buyers understand they were buying leasehold rather than fee interests? Indeed, the answer to these last two questions is "they should have." Thus, one can argue that governments shouldn't be favoring one side against the other in this private dispute over clearly defined property rights.

However, tens of thousands of owner-occupants of leasehold single-family houses and condominiums in Hawaii constitute a powerful interest group that elected officials simply cannot ignore. When the proverbial gorilla asks for your lunch, it's hard to say no. In this case, it was someone else's lunch and that made the outcome even more predictable. Government surely would have stayed out of this matter

The duck stops here

if only a few lessees had been involved or if the property in question had been anything but voters' homes. There is something upsetting about owners being forced out of their homes.

There also is a sound economic reason for eliminating leasehold housing, even where landowners are unwilling to sell. In the political fight over who will gain the benefits of land price appreciation, both landowners and lessees already have spent countless hours and millions of dollars in public relations, lobbying and legal fees. Their expenditures represent pure economic waste since none of these efforts increased total production or income in Hawaii. These resources surely could have been spent more productively. Unfortunately, as long as leasehold residential housing remains a significant feature of housing in Hawaii, these unproductive activities will continue. Forcing landowners to sell is the quickest (but perhaps not the fairest) way to end them once and for all.

Alternatives. Are there alternatives to involuntary conversion?

Some suggest rent control on land, which would benefit lessees at the expense of landowners. This would especially appeal to lessees with little interest in buying, such as many retirees. Land-rent control already is available to owners of leasehold single-family homes, but it has not solved the problem of increasingly unaffordable land rents. And it is not available at all to owners of condominiums, co-ops and town homes. The Honolulu City Council passed a ground-rent control measure in 1991 which Bishop Estate also has challenged in court.

Critics of rent control argue that it would depress economic returns to landlords and thus discourage the development of housing. This argument has long been used against the regulation of apartment rents. There is, however, a major difference between the regulation of apartment rents and the regulation of rents on land under housing. The depression of economic returns to rental apartment owners after the imposition of rent control would indeed induce potential investors to steer clear of rental apartments; the supply of rental housing would thus be reduced. By contrast, the supply of land cannot be reduced by rent control since the land is already there. Lease-rent control also would encourage landowners to convert their leasehold-residential land to fee simple without resorting to costly condemnation proceedings.

Aside from the basic question of fairness, the major problem with land-rent control is the high cost of administering the program. The bureaucratic machinery needed to settle disputes, determine the initial lease rents and subsequent market rents at renegotiation, and certify eligibility for the program is likely to use larger amounts of public resources than proponents envision. Also, since mortgage interest is tax deductible while lease rents are not, leasehold increases the cost of housing to homeowners.

Why should the State and local governments help residential-land lessees in Hawaii buy their land outright? Simply because leasehold-residential housing increases the cost of housing, inevitably encourages unproductive self-serving activities, and, in the long run, is politically untenable.

CHAPTER 30

NATIVE HAWAIIAN CLAIMS

H.K. BRUSS KEPPELER, ESQ.
Lyons Brandt Cook & Hiramatsu

"Why would the State pay over $100 million in damages to Hawaiians and go along with demands for 'sovereignty'?"

Some of the issues are pretty complex but (1) Hawaiians are legally and morally entitled to much more than the $100 million-plus they are likely to receive from the State, (2) sovereignty is not as crazy as it may sound, and (3) it will happen.

Don't go blaming the present administration and legislators. To really understand what happened and why the taxpayers of today and tomorrow are getting stuck for the tab, you have to go *way* back.

The root cause. Ho'okipa, in a sense, was the root cause. This Hawaiian value translates to hospitality of the *highest order*. In ancient days, it applied to members of the same 'ohana or when kama'āina (old timers) entertained malihini (newcomers). When haole (at first Caucasians, later other races) began arriving, conflict was inevitable. These malihini were welcomed with full-on ho'okipa, without any inkling of how their Western mores would clash with Hawaiian values.

At first, I'm sure, this hospitality was accepted graciously and little thought was given to its implications, but all that changed about the time that the first foreigner realized the strategic advantage and economic viability of these islands.

If space permitted, I would tell you a number of stories: there would be the one about King Kamehameha III in 1843, with the guns of H.M.S. *Caryfort* trained on him, relinquishing his kingdom to its commander, Lord George Paulet; another would portray Hawaii as an anything-goes R & R stop for New England whalers tuckered out from slaughtering whales. I might add a very sad one about a Hawaiian population, conservatively put at 200,000 in 1778, plunging to 34,000 by 1893; another would involve the fortunes made in Hawaii by haole businessmen during the gold rush years when Hawaii was California's breadbasket, and even bigger fortunes made when sugar could be sold for top dollar to the North during the American Civil War. I would want to detail what these same businessmen did to King Kalākaua when he was so audacious as to suggest that their profits should be taxed more heavily. Mind you, these are just a few of the stories I could tell. They don't begin to provide the whole story of exploitation visited upon Hawaiians since the arrival of Captain Cook.

Some people blame the Hawaiians for having let others run roughshod over them. Well, I guess that just brings us back to ho'okipa, and to the clash of Hawaiian values with Western mores. To ask how the Hawaiians could allow this to happen is a bit like asking how Bambi's mother could have allowed the hunter to shoot her.

"But that's ancient history. Why make a big deal of it now?"

I could answer that in many ways. I happen to be a lawyer, so I'm going to focus on the legal analysis.

First, crimes have been committed. Like most crimes, these were about money and passion—particularly about sugar fortunes, tariffs and "American Destiny." By 1887, an unfamiliar Western political system and a new land-title regime had been superimposed on the Kingdom. King Kalākaua was balking at the latest demands of the haole business-men. What they *really* wanted was annexation by the United States to get around sugar import tariffs. But, aware of popular opposition to annexation, they sought a renewal of the Reciprocity Treaty which let Hawaiian sugar into the U.S. duty-free. The U.S. Government wanted Pearl Harbor in exchange for the treaty's extension. The King refused.

So, in January of 1887, a "Hawaiian League" was formed and by midyear membership had grown to about 400. The few part-Hawaiian members were far outnumbered by Americans, English, Germans and Portuguese. Orientals were barred from membership. Also in 1887 the Honolulu Rifles, a para-military group of foreign nationals, built up its membership and prepared for battle.

"Bayonet Constitution." On July 6, while the Rifles patrolled the streets outside the palace with bayonets fixed, the League's leaders confronted King Kalákaua and forced him to sign a new constitution. This "Bayonet Constitution" truncated the powers of the monarch, established property ownership as a voting qualification (thus disenfranchising most Hawaiians), and allowed foreign noncitizen residents to vote so long as they could demonstrate their understanding of the constitution in English, a language foreign to most Hawaiians. When Lili'uokalani ascended to the throne in 1891, the Hawaiian political base was so eroded that a Western takeover was inevitable.

During the spring of 1892, the annexationists and the resident U.S. Minister, John L. Stevens, hatched a plot to overthrow the Queen. Among other overt acts, they wrote to the U.S. Secretary of State, stressing the strategic advantages of annexation. All that was needed was a convenient excuse to take action.

On January 14, 1893, at the end of a frustrating and unfruitful session of the legislature, Queen Lili'uokalani announced to the cabinet that she would proclaim a new constitution restoring some of the monarch's powers stripped away by the Bayonet Constitution, and restricting voting to those born in Hawai'i or naturalized. This was the opportunity the annexationists wanted. A "Committee of Safety" of 13 men took it upon itself to declare that the actions of the Queen were *revolutionary*. Of the 13, none was Hawaiian and only seven were citizens of Hawai'i!

The Queen yields and appeals. In three short days, it was all over. American troops had landed from the U.S.S. *Boston*; a provisional government, formed by the 13 non-Hawaiians (without so much as an attempt to organize a vote of the people), had been recognized by the U.S. Minister; and the Queen, in carefully phrased words, had agreed to "yield to the superior force of the United States ... to avoid any collision of armed forces and perhaps the loss of life." The Queen immediately appealed to the President of the United States expecting, as had been the experience of Kamehameha III in 1843, to secure the return of Hawaiian sovereignty.

President Grover Cleveland responded by sending James H. Blount of Georgia, former chairman of the House Committee on Foreign Affairs, to investigate. Blount reported that the so-called revolution was caused by the dissatisfaction of a small group of white businessmen; that without the interference of the U.S. Minister (not to mention the U.S. Navy), there could not have been a revolution; and that a majority of both native and white residents favored a monarchy. President Cleveland was appalled by what he read and strongly expressed his support for the Queen in a message to a U.S. Congress that did nothing. The annexationists simply waited until Cleveland was out of office and William McKinley was in before seeking annexation again in 1898 ... this time successfully. (Ever wonder why there is a McKinley Street and a McKinley High School, but no Cleveland *anything* in Hawai'i?)

In 1895, Robert Wilcox, a part-Hawaiian, instigated a counter-revolution aimed at restoring the monarchy. It was quickly put down and about 200 Hawaiians and haole sympathizers were arrested. Queen Lili'uokalani, forced to abdicate, was fined and imprisoned.

> *"All the foregoing may be true, but could anyone even begin to untangle the current situation in such a way that all fruits of these crimes could be returned to their rightful owners?*
> *Shouldn't we let bygones be bygones?"*

Wait, there's more to the story.

The U.S. Congress in 1921 established the "Hawaiian Homes" program, a land trust of roughly 200,000 acres for homesteading by persons of 50 percent or more Hawaiian blood. But sugar interests conditioned their support of this legislation on exclusion of the prime agricultural land they were using. As a result, the homestead trust

consisted largely of the worst land in the territory. Also, opponents of Hawaiian Homes insisted that the homestead program be self-support-ing, without direct federal assistance. Lacking funds, most of the land just sat there.

Breached duty. During the territorial years, some egregious breaches of fiduciary duty were committed. Thousands of acres of homestead land were transferred to federal and territorial agencies by executive orders and proclamations of federally appointed territorial governors. In the end, 29,633 acres were lost. In addition, vast Hawaiian Home acreage was leased at pittances to private sugar and ranching interests, leaving little to homestead even if there had been money to build necessary infrastructure. These breaches and other failures in the administration of the program are well-documented in reports of federal agencies. The Federal-State Task Force on the Hawaiian Homes Commission Act Report (August 1983), for example, lists 134 major infractions.

At the time of statehood (1959), the federal government transferred administration of the homestead program to the new State of Hawaii, retaining only "oversight" responsibilities. At one time, the federal government viewed itself as a "co-trustee" of the program, but in recent years it has claimed otherwise.

"So why haven't Hawaiians sued?"

Under the Hawai'i Admission Act, only the United States itself can bring suit in federal court for breaches of the homestead trust and no suit has ever been filed. At the state level, Hawaiians have sued ... and won.

In 1988, realizing that these controversies would not just go away, and not wanting them to fester any longer, the State Legislature required the governor to present a proposal for resolution of the controversies which had developed since statehood. Governor John Waihee submitted an action plan in 1991. In February 1992, a task force recommended to the legislature that $12 million be appropriated to pay back rents for state use of Hawaiian Home lands since statehood, and that future use be compensated under general leases or by land exchange.

One reason that amount is low is the difficulty in establishing with any degree of precision the exact amount of damages. The range of possibilities is wide and the report opts for a number at the low end. I hate to sound like a complainer, but this goes against the grain of established trust law. When a fiduciary duty has been breached (and everyone agrees that such duties have been repeatedly breached), any uncertainty in the calculation of damages is supposed to be resolved against the fiduciary.

Whatever the State finally decides to pay, it will be peanuts compared to the next little matter.

The Ceded Lands Trust. At the time of statehood, another important trust was created. Under the Admission Act, 1.2 million acres of the land ceded to the United States by the Republic of Hawai'i was ceded back to the State of Hawai'i. The income derived from this land was to be used for five stated purposes, including "the betterment of the conditions of Native Hawaiians."

Until 1980, however, not one penny of this income ever made its way to these intended beneficiaries. The Office of Hawaiian Affairs (OHA) was funded in 1980 and, for the first time, ceded-land income began to benefit Hawaiians directly. Not until 1990, however, was the full extent of this income determined.

Negotiations between OHA and the State for a settlement of unpaid benefits continued through early 1992 when it was announced that the settlement would be for $111.8 million. At this writing the amount is being reviewed, but it is contemplated that the settlement will be paid—some in cash, the rest in land.

Let's summarize. The Kingdom of Hawai'i was illegally overthrown with the direct assistance of the U.S. Government, and the trustees of the several trusts established by the U.S. Government for the benefit of Hawaiians have repeatedly breached their fiduciary duties.

Is it any surprise that Hawaiians want more than apologies and social services? The fact of the matter is that many want more than just money and land; they want political autonomy.

Hawaiian Sovereignty. Recently initiatives for a restored sovereign Hawaiian nation have emerged. At least one envisions a sovereign and independent Hawai'i. Another sees a "nation within a nation" with status similar to that of the 308 Indian Tribal and Alaskan Native Nations that already exist within of the United States.

The Reagan and Bush administrations inadvertently pressured Hawaiians into thinking more seriously about sovereignty by formally rejecting federal funding of the Hawaiian Homes program on the basis that it would require illegal preferences based on racial classification, as distinguished from the constitutional authority to benefit "Native Americans as members of [tribal nations]." If this position is correct, Hawaiians *must* have sovereignty!

In early 1991, Hui Na'auao, a coalition of more than 40 organizations representing the full spectrum of Hawaiian political thought, from conservative to self-proclaimed radical, was formed to seek a grant from the U.S. Administration for Native Americans. Hui Na'auao is embarking on a remarkable odyssey in search of a form of sovereignty, self-determination and self-governance Hawaiians can choose for themselves. Under any scenario, the land base for the new nation will surely incorporate the tracts set aside for the Hawaiian Home Land

"YOU PEOPLE SHOULD HAVE PULLED YOURSELVES UP BY YOUR BOOTSTRAPS BY NOW..."

Trust and at least a portion of the Ceded Lands Trust. If the "nation within a nation" option is chosen, there may be an attempt to consolidate, but more likely it will retain a "checkerboard" pattern. Just as you don't really know now whether you're on ceded land, you wouldn't necessarily know when you were on land of the new sovereign nation.

During deliberations over the Hawaiian Homes legislation in 1920, then Governor Charles J. McCarthy wrote: "Personally, I have my doubts as to whether the Act will do all that is claimed, but I am strongly in favor of it and I am willing to give it all the support I can. If it works it will be the best thing that could possibly happen to the Hawaiians and also the Territory at large. Should it fail the Hawaiian people will have only themselves to blame."

If Hawaiians are to be blamed for the failure of programs always administered by others, perhaps it is time for them to determine their own destiny. In a monumental clash of cultures over which they have had no control, Hawaiians continue to dominate the "bad lists" in criminal justice, health, education and welfare. It is sadly ironic that in many ways this is a direct result of their traditions of ho'okipa and aloha. It's as if their lunch keeps getting eaten by others, and then they are blamed for being malnourished.

The trust assets represented by the Hawaiian Home Land and Ceded Lands trusts should place Hawaiians among the wealthiest people in the United States. Despite this, they are the poorest, the sickest and the least educated of the State of Hawai'i.

With any luck, the many breaches of trust will be settled, Hawaiians will be given political and economic autonomy, and the land of Aloha can truly begin to heal its wounds.

CHAPTER 31

WOMEN & JOBS

CORALIE CHUN MATAYOSHI, ESQ.
Executive Director
Hawaii State Bar Association

"Do women in Hawaii have equal access to jobs?"

Back in 1873, there was no question about the role of women. "The paramount destiny and mission of woman are to fulfill the noble and benign offices of wife and mother," decreed the all-male Supreme Court of the United States in denying women admittance to the practice of law.

Women eventually challenged this time-honored tenet by entering the work force in record numbers. Their entry was facilitated by the mechanization of factories which reduced the necessity for physical strength in industrial jobs. The growth in clerical needs and service industries drew still more women into the work force. By 1945, one-third of the workers in America were women.

A similar phenomenon occurred in Hawaii, starting in the 1950s. With the post-World War II rise in tourism and the decline of sugar and pineapple, service industry jobs burgeoned. Spurred by a higher cost of living, women took advantage of these opportunities. In 1950, 23 percent of the women in Hawaii worked outside the home. By 1990, the percentage had grown to 61 percent.

More enter professions. The establishment of medical and law schools in Hawaii in the mid-1970s enhanced the opportunity for more women to enter into business, law, medicine, government and other professional fields. The first graduating class from the University of Hawaii School of Law in 1976 led the nation with 35 percent females. In recent years the percentage has been above 50 percent.

Today, almost exactly half of Hawaii's work force is female. But how far have women come in terms of equality in the workplace?

One objective measure of equality is pay. Another is hiring, promotion and retention practices. What is amazing about pay equity is the lack of it. In the half century between 1930 and 1980, although the number of women in the work force tripled, average female earnings nationally never got higher than 59 percent of average male earnings. The disparity has not been as great in Hawaii, but our numbers are nothing to brag about.

Women underpaid. Today, the average woman in Hawaii receives only 65 cents for every dollar the average man earns. Overrepresented in lower-paying jobs, women earn consistently less than men across virtually all job categories. Studies have shown that differences in education, work experience and other objective factors account only partly for the wage gap. Estimates of the gap attributable to discrimination range from 23 percent to 56 percent.

The wage gap is significant in two professions where one would least expect to find discrimination. A 1991 survey done for the Hawaii State Bar Association by SMS Research found the average income of women attorneys to be only 58 percent of male attorneys'. Even when factors such as age, years in practice, and position are constant, women still make significantly less than men.

A 1991 preliminary faculty-pay-equity study conducted for the University of Hawaii at Manoa (UH) by Professors Kiyoshi Ikeda and Linda Johnsrud found that—other factors being equal—female faculty members at UH make $126 to $144 a month (about $1,700 a year) less than their male counterparts.

Statistics regarding other objective measures of equality similarly offer little consolation. Women hold only 9.1 percent of corporate directorships for the top 50 Hawaii companies. But at least this percentage has been climbing. The percentage of women CEOs and Board Chairs in Hawaii has actually slipped in the past eight years, from

2.9 percent to 1.9 percent!

Glass ceiling. The fact that the highest echelons of business in Hawaii are dominated by older males may keep women from rising to their full potential. It's called a glass ceiling—impossible to see, but effective nonetheless. Moreover, if Japanese interests continue to pervade Hawaii's economy, the relative lack of success of Japanese women in climbing the corporate ladder portends an even more ominous barrier to Hawaii women trying to make it to the top.

In the legal profession, the 1991 Hawaii State Bar Association survey found that women are less likely to be partners or supervisors (33.7 percent of the female attorneys hold such positions compared to 48 percent of the male attorneys). And, while over 25 percent of the active lawyers in Hawaii are women, none has graced the federal bench in Hawaii, and only one (Rhoda Lewis from 1959 to 1967) has served on the Hawaii Supreme Court in modern times.

Another 1991 study on barriers to retention and tenure at UH conducted by Professor Johnsrud concluded that structural discrimination (such as lack of support for gender-related research and maternity-leave policies) and personal discrimination (sexual harassment, stereotyping and tokenism) are perceived by faculty women as barriers to their progress.

"Old boys network." A 1992 national study by the Center for Women in Government found that Hawaii women had the nation's lowest participation rate in senior state and local government posts (13.9 percent). Contrast this phenomenon with the fact that Hawaii has at times led the nation in the number of women holding elective office at the state and county level. One senses that women are more successful in pursuing their fullest potential when judged by Hawaii voters than by the closely guarded "old boys network" that controls government and business.

What can government do to help the situation? The Hawaii State Legislature already has done quite a bit. Hawaii was the first state to ratify the Equal Rights Amendment to the United States Constitution, and the first to enact an identical provision to its own constitution.

Hawaii's law prohibiting sex discrimination in employment contains more prohibited categories of discrimination than that of most states, and more than the federal Civil Rights Act of 1964.

Hawaii was one of the first states to recognize women's reproductive rights, and its laws are among the most liberal in the nation on maternity-leave policies. Female employees disabled due to pregnancy, childbirth or related medical conditions are permitted to take a leave of absence for a "reasonable amount of time" (i.e., whatever is medically necessary, as determined by her doctor). Federal law simply treats pregnancy like any other disability. Hawaii also has its own comprehensive Equal Pay Act to complement the federal Equal Pay Act.

Discrimination hard to prove. While these laws are important and progressive, they have not always worked the way they are supposed to. Part of the problem is that most discrimination is subtle and difficult to prove. Unless a woman is fired, there is little incentive to endure the emotional and financial cost often needed to file a grievance.

Some attempts have been made to evaluate jobs on a point scale so that the value of a nurse, for example, can be compared to the value of, say, a truck driver. "Comparable worth" is considered by many to be an important step toward pay equality. Unfortunately, it is somewhat subjective and fraught with high levels of disagreement and debate.

In 1986, through the persistence of numerous women and community groups, the Hawaii State Legislature addressed this issue by authorizing a pay-equity study of public employment. The consultants, Arthur Young & Co., found "differences" in the way officials assign wages to jobs filled largely by women and those occupied primarily by men. As a result of their recommendations, the legislature appropriated $850,000 to cover salary adjustments to rectify the differences. Additional job classes were supposed to have been reviewed for adjustments, but little more was ever done.

Looking to ourselves. Ironically, the root of these problems and the solutions lie within ourselves—in the way men perceive women and how women view themselves. Women have ventured into the work force in great numbers, yet many in society still view the primary role of women as the U.S. Supreme Court viewed it back in 1873—to serve the "noble and benign offices of wife and mother." Women themselves often feel guilty about pursuing a demanding career that prevents them from being a "good" mother and wife. And even the most liberal man would probably ask his wife to cut back on her career before hurting his own if two demanding careers proved detrimental to their family life.

Herein lies the dilemma which nearly all of Hawaii's women face during their lifetimes. The already high and still rising cost of living here requires women at all economic levels to serve as either sole breadwinners (as in the case of the divorced, widowed or deliberately-single parent) or equal partners in bringing home the bacon. At the same time, society continues to demand that women bear most, if not all, of the burden of family care giving. (Given that Hawaii has the highest longevity rates in the nation, even women without children will increasingly need to assume the role of care giver for elderly parents.)

As long as women are asked to do it all (and even if they succeed), their quality of life will suffer. While each woman may begin a personal social revolution toward equality at home, the most effective impetus for changing society's overall expectations of women will actually begin in the workplace, by a new generation of men and women at the top.

Thankfully, the wheels of change already are in motion. Medical, law, business and other schools of higher education are turning out record numbers of women doctors, lawyers, MBA's and other professionals (36 percent of UH medical school graduates, 55 percent of UH law school graduates and 43 percent of UH MBA recipients are female). These young, educated women are working side by side with male colleagues generally more open to gender equality than their fathers were.

Only when society in general, and particularly those in power, truly understand and internalize the burdens women face, will we be able to put our collective hearts and minds into making concepts such as equal pay for equal work, equitable promotion and retention policies, and comparable worth a part of everyday life for all people of Hawaii.

CHAPTER 32

PUBLIC SCHOOLS

JOHN P. DOLLY
Dean and Professor of Education
College of Education
University of Hawaii

"Why are the test scores of public school children so low?"

Hawaii faces the same challenges the rest of the nation does in trying to provide a quality education to a complex mix of students. Public education in general is a system problem more than a people problem.

Hawaii's public school system was designed a hundred years ago for a population whose needs differed from those of today's students. Changing demographics are requiring schools to do more. They are expected to lift students to a higher level of competence, and to accomplish this while reducing the time students spend in school and the level of public support. In effect, we have a system that is doomed to failure.

Asking the wrong question. We worry too much about test scores. Clearly, the issue of who is being tested is important. An exceptionally high percentage of Hawaii's students attend private schools (between 17 and 18 percent compared to a national average of only 11 percent). Comparisons to national data can be misleading. Also, people need to remember that standardized tests do not measure what a student is capable of actually doing in the real world. To find that out we need performance assessment. Schools engage in little performance assessment. Worrying about a student's standardized test score seems irrelevant, particularly for the large number who have no intention of ever going on to higher education.

To put it bluntly, we keep asking the wrong questions in education. We need to ask, "What can students do after they complete a certain level of education?" Schools should spell out explicitly what they prepare students to do, and what they guarantee their graduates will be able to do.

Most European systems require students to attend school for at least 220 days a year. In Hawaii, students attend for 180 days. Even on those 180 days, one would be hard pressed to guarantee that students were on-task the entire time. Making a comparison between a Hawaii student who goes to school 180 days with a 220-day European student is simply not fair. The comparison gets even more distorted when one compares Hawaii students with those from Japan.

I had the opportunity to meet with teachers and principals in Japan in 1991. Based on those conversations, I calculated that when private after-school and weekend classes are considered, the typical Japanese middle-school student spends the equivalent of 300 Hawaiian school days in class. It doesn't take a rocket scientist to figure out that the student who spends 300 days a year in school is likely to learn more than one who spends 180 days there.

There are things we can do to improve public education in Hawaii. However, our safest bet is to start over. The changes that most people talk about are minor: extending the school day a little, more rigorous standards for teachers, getting parents more heavily involved, and developing school-based management. Nobody talks about holding anybody in the system accountable for performance, including the students.

Increase accountability. Here are several steps that should be taken to improve public education in Hawaii. The **Department of Education** must guarantee that students completing certain grade levels will be certified on the basis of performance rather than meaningless test scores and meaningless grades. **Teachers** must be held accountable for the quality of instruction they deliver and the performance of their students. **Principals** need to be held accountable to parents, teachers and students for their leadership and instructional support. **Students** need to be held accountable for their behavior and their performance in schools.

Students in some schools are so disruptive they are ruining the learning environment for other students. Schools must be free to remove them to give the majority a supportive environment free of distractions. The schools need an *enforced* code of student conduct.

Parents must be accountable and responsive to the schools; they simply cannot dump their children on the school steps and expect teachers to solve all their problems. The **School Board** must clearly state what schools are capable and willing to do and what they are not capable of doing. We are making schools centers for social services and that's fine, but the appropriate people must provide these services. We simply cannot expect teachers to do it all. If students need social-work support, then social workers need to be placed in schools; if they need medical assistance, then nurses or other medical personnel are called for.

"BUT I HAD NO IDEA WE WERE THE MOST VIOLENT IN THE NATION..."

Good people work in our public schools, some of the finest teachers in the country. The problem is that Hawaii doesn't have enough of them. Hawaii has a teacher shortage that may further undermine the quality of education. Teacher shortages often lead to short-circuit programs for certification. They also lead to teachers' teaching outside their fields. When large numbers do that, the quality of education offered to students declines.

Keep government out. The government has no business intruding into the individual classroom—an unfortunately common practice in this state. I have witnessed the legislature debate what subjects should be offered in a high school, and whether certain programs should be mandated. No wonder we have problems in public education in Hawaii, when legislators are telling the schools what they should and shouldn't be doing. These policy decisions need to be made by the school board. If we want to improve the quality of education, get the legislature out of the classroom.

One problem I see as we try to improve Hawaii's education is the closed system we have developed. In order to become an administrator, you must come up through Hawaii's system. This closes off the introduction of outside leadership, new ideas, and new initiatives, and tends to clone people. You follow the leader or you are not supported for an administrative position. Other U.S. school districts bring in principals, superintendents and other school leaders from the outside. They have new ideas and new perspectives, and will look at things differently. Hawaii seems to fear the unknown. We also think we know what's best for us and that we don't need ideas from the Mainland. This closed-mindedness does nothing to encourage innovation or creativity in our schools.

Make schools compete. We must remember that the public schools in Hawaii, like those in the rest of the country, are monopolies, not likely to change quickly. It's time to make schools compete. Let's open the system to allow greater flexibility at the school level and greater decision making for parents. The success of several centers of excellence in our high schools illustrates that schools have the potential to be creative and supportive of students. The movement toward school-based management will allow more of this.

We need a simplified system for applying for and granting district exceptions. If some public schools go out of business, so be it. Some may need to go. People are paying taxes; they should be able to choose the school they want their son or daughter to attend.

Certain neighborhoods have substandard schools. It's true and it helps no one to pretend that it isn't. We ought to give those people an opportunity to let their sons and daughters go elsewhere. Without competition and without accountability we are not going to see much change in public education in Hawaii or anywhere else.

A few other items can have a positive impact on education in Hawaii. One simple technique is not allowing schools to get too large. There is enough evidence now on the Mainland to conclude that large schools create more problems than they are worth. We should create schools within schools where students are known, have an identity, and where a clearly defined group of teachers is responsible for them. Creating a sense of community in the schools is a lot easier when you are dealing with smaller numbers.

Bizarre tradition. Another problem in Hawaii is our bizarre tradition of allowing principals to belong to a union. If principals are

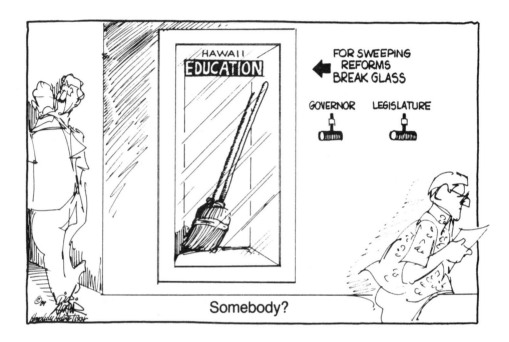

to lead, they need to be out of the union, exercising leadership. If they are so insecure that they need a tenure base to fall back on, we should look to the model at the University of Hawaii where administrators can retain their tenure as teachers. But *no one* should have tenure in an administrative position.

Equally frustrating is the fact that the State of Hawaii has a unified school system. When teachers get tenure, it's in the entire system. This allows them to migrate freely from school to school. If we want to create stability in rural schools and neighbor island districts, it is critical that we stop this practice. Grant teachers tenure, but only for their district or their geographic location. If they wish to move to Honolulu, they should have to apply for positions as they become available, and start the tenure and probationary process over in their new location.

Change won't be cheap. What is all this going to cost? Plenty. You need to increase the number of school days—that means raising principals' and teachers' compensation. It means additional costs for utilities and school maintenance, and money would have to be allocated to allow the schools time to restructure.

We also must create a greater commitment to public education. A sure sign the system is in trouble is the fact that professional people have by and large abandoned Hawaii's public schools. Even more distressing is the fact that large numbers of public school teachers and administrators send their own children to private schools. That's one hell of an indictment.

RAINBOW STADIUM

CORKY

"THEN EVERYBODY WANTED A SAY IN THE SEARCH FOR A NEW U.H. PRESIDENT..."

CHAPTER 33

UNIVERSITY OF HAWAII

SUMNER J. LA CROIX
Professor of Economics
University of Hawaii

"Can a student get a good education at the University of Hawaii at Manoa?"

To get right to the point, "yes". A good student can get a good education at the University of Hawaii at Manoa (which I usually call UH). It's no surprise that *Money* magazine recently identified UH as one of the nation's top colleges for the money. Tuition is affordable ($615 per semester in 1992) compared to both private and public universities on the Mainland, and students from Oahu can cut expenses by living at home. Yet, in spite of the University's many strong academic programs, students often graduate from UH with mediocre educations. The blame lies with all major players — faculty, administration and students.

UH, founded as a land-grant college in 1907, remained small and limited in scope until Governors Quinn (1959-1962) and Burns (1962-1973) dramatically increased the share of state revenues allocated to the university. By 1972 the UH budget had increased to 15.53 percent of the state budget. The dramatic increases in UH funding came to an abrupt halt in the 1970s during Governor Ariyoshi's administration (1973-1986). Between 1972 and 1980 the UH budget, adjusted for inflation, actually fell by more than 10 percent. Faculty salaries became uncompetitive, and many excellent professors left for better-paying mainland universities. The morale of faculty and students was low, and the university seemed (at least to this writer who arrived as an assistant professor in 1981) to be anything but a dynamic institution.

Support during the 1980s. The downward slide stopped in 1980, and inflation-adjusted expenditures on UH increased by almost 4.5 percent a year over the 1981-1990 decade. The actual increase was even larger, as funding for extensive campus construction was included in the State's capital budget. In fiscal year 1989 (the most recent year for which comparison statistics are available) state per-capita expenditures on higher education were 21.3 percent above the national average. This places Hawaii eighteenth in the country and suggests that any problems at UH are not necessarily the result of inadequate state funding.

UH has a solid faculty, and the restoration of faculty salaries to more competitive levels in recent years should help to retain them. Some top-notch UH faculty members could move to a top-30 university, but stay because they enjoy living in Hawaii, have a unique research environment (such as clear skies on Mauna Kea), have easy travel access to Asia, or have colleagues who also specialize in Hawaiian, Asian and Pacific studies.

At many mainland state universities (the University of Washington at Seattle is one), undergraduate students have little access to the faculty during their freshman and sophomore years. Introductory classes are extremely large (500-800 students), many classes are handled by teaching assistants, and appointments with leading professors are difficult to arrange. By contrast, undergraduates at Manoa often have classes with the best faculty, introductory classes are 50 to 200 in most cases, almost all undergraduate classes are taught by regular faculty, and professors are generally accessible and willing to see students.

Why then did a 1991 poll of 1986 UH graduates identify "apathetic students and instructors" as the most disappointing aspect of UH? A major problem is that the university pays little attention to how the faculty teaches. The administration has allocated funds to a new Center for Teaching Excellence, but it has had little impact on faculty teaching so far and the administration uses few carrots or sticks to motivate faculty. There are only a smattering of tangible rewards for good teaching, and the University makes little effort to monitor the quality of faculty teaching. It's no surprise that some professors prefer to emphasize research or their tennis game over teaching.

Still, every department has good teachers. If a student is willing to spend time finding out which professors and which courses are high quality, he or she can obtain a good education. Many prominent private and public universities facilitate student search for good courses and professors by editing and publishing student evaluations. At UH, however, the official student evaluations are confidential. Currently enrolled students can't find out how previous students evaluated the professor. Consequently, UH students are severely handicapped by lack of information on courses and faculty. The administration could quickly improve education at UH by publishing a booklet of edited student evaluations.

Shortcomings. Perhaps that story is indicative of a larger problem: a failure to provide services to students which would facilitate a good education. Few student advisors are available, although the legislature has increased funding for them in recent years. Hamilton Library has far too little study space, and job placement services are markedly deficient. A severe shortage of campus housing forces many students to commute long distances daily and little student parking is provided for the commuters. Any student not from a neighbor island has little chance of getting a dorm room—only 2 percent of undergraduate women and 10 percent of undergraduate men are housed in dormitories. Most UH students leave the campus after their classes. Consequently, campus activity is a pale shadow of the rich life found at many mainland universities.

All of these factors help to explain why many UH professors insist that their own children attend mainland colleges. UH offers a good academic education, but fails to offer the student the opportunities which make attending an excellent university a transforming experience.

This brings us to UH's student body. When I recently asked

students in my introductory macroeconomics class why they enrolled, the overwhelming majority cited the class time and college requirements. Fewer than 10 percent of the students had gathered more specific information about me or the course. So why is the time slot for the class so important? At UH 90.3 percent of undergraduates have jobs, compared to 62.3 percent at mainland universities. In addition, conversations with my students lead me to believe that UH students work more hours than mainland students do. Time slots for classes are important to students who often want to bunch their classes in the morning so they can leave campus for their jobs in the afternoon. Working students typically have too little time to study, spend too little time on campus, and have too little interaction with other students.

Poor preparation. The problem of working students is compounded by the poor academic preparation many received in Hawaii's public schools. The average combined Scholastic Aptitude Test (SAT) score of incoming UH students is 12 percent better than the average for all Hawaii test takers, and 10 percent above the U.S. average. This may sound respectable, but it is a deplorable record for a state's flagship university. A comparison with the average SAT scores from a few mainland schools is instructive. (Some Western schools are not included in Table 1 because they either do not report average SAT scores or use the ACT rather than the SAT.)

Table 1

School	Average Combined SAT
Univ. of Virginia	1,208
UC-Berkeley	1,197
Univ. of Wisconsin	1,099
Florida State Univ.	1,097
Univ. of Colorado	1,070
Univ. of Arizona	1,050
UC-Davis	1,050
Univ. of Washington	1,035
Univ. of Delaware	1,031
Univ. of Oregon	1,003
Univ. of Hawaii at Manoa	**980**
Univ. of Idaho	980

The UH freshmen's relatively low average SAT score indicates that many need additional study time if they are to achieve academic excellence. Too few, however, put forth the needed extra effort, as the combined effects of commuting and long hours on a job leave harried students little time or energy.

The combination of mixed faculty teaching, meager support services for students, poor preparation in high school, and too much student time spent on the freeway and on the job produces disappointing results. For example, 48 percent of the UH undergraduates who recently took the national Law School Admission Test (LSAT) earned scores in the top half of all test takers—by far the best showing of any college or university in Hawaii, but still stacking up poorly against the performances of undergraduates at other states' flagship universities. Table 2 lists the percentages from a few such mainland schools.

Table 2

School	Percentage of Graduates In Top Half of LSAT
Univ. of Virginia	79
Univ. of Colorado	71
Univ. of Wisconsin	71
Univ. of Washington	70
Univ. of Iowa	69
Univ. of Florida	66
Univ. of Kansas	65
Univ. of Missouri	65
Univ. of Oregon	64
Univ. of Utah	63
Univ. of Montana	61
Univ. of Arizona	60
Univ. of Idaho	60
Univ. of Hawaii at Manoa	**48**

This comparison suggests that UH is not doing a good job educating its students. Perhaps one reason for the poor performance is a certain provincialism at UH. Only 7 percent of undergraduate students are from the Mainland. If UH could attract more academically excellent students (possibly with reciprocal admission agreements with other state universities), students from Hawaii would be productively exposed to a broader cross section of the U.S. population. The University of Virginia is a good example of a state university that admits a large percentage of academically excellent students from outside Virginia who significantly improve the quality of its academic programs.

As long as students are spending more time on the freeway and on the job than at the university, many can forget about achieving academic excellence. If, however, a student makes the time commitment required to succeed in school and selects courses and professors carefully, that student *can* get a good education at UH. But *do* most students at UH get a good education?

Many motivated students get an excellent education; some are sandbagged by the lack of student services at UH; and others are unwilling to make the time commitments needed to succeed in school. Unless UH and its students both reexamine and change their priorities, the University of Hawaii at Manoa will be known as a good school for the money rather than as a good school.

CHAPTER 34

AIRPORT EXPANSION

BILL WOOD
Editor
Hawaii Investor Magazine

"Why are we spending billions to expand the Honolulu Airport?"

The airports development plan, approved by the State in 1990, will involve about $2.5 billion of construction by 1996. Most of that is going toward new terminals and other expansion at Honolulu International Airport, in a section of urban Oahu where three massive public works projects now are under way. Scheduled to start late in 1992 for completion in 1997 is the $1.7 billion Honolulu rapid transit system, a 15-mile-long elevated railway whose 22 stations will include one at the airport. In the brick-red hills just above the airport, the new H-3 freeway punches through the Koolau Mountains to connect Leeward Honolulu with rural Windward Oahu. When it's completed in 1993, that project will have cost federal and state taxpayers $850 million.

In a perfect world, these projects eventually would be paid for by those who use them, either through direct user fees, such as the fares to be charged rapid transit passengers, or special taxes. This is not going to happen. Still, that doesn't stop local government from borrowing the money to pay for them on the far more solid theory that if the projects don't generate the cash to pay back the loans, the taxpayers will.

Of the billions being spent on Oahu, nowhere are the costs more concentrated than at Honolulu International Airport, where three new terminals are being built. First to be completed will be an interisland terminal, serving intrastate flights. Then comes the overseas terminal, to handle flights to and from the U.S. Mainland. The largest and centerpiece of the program is the new international terminal. It will contain more than 1.5 million square feet of floor space, the size of Ala Moana Center.

Necessary expansion? State officials, from Governor John Waihee down, say that a new international terminal is needed to handle the growing number of foreign visitors that have become an important market for Hawaii's tourism industry.

Passengers arriving from Japan have had to spend up to three hours clearing customs—certainly an unpleasant beginning to their visit. But much of the delay has been the result of a shortage of U.S. customs agents. That's being corrected, in any event, with increases in customs service staffing. So now the problem is said to be a shortage of facilities. That's the main argument supporting the huge, half-billion-dollar international terminal.

This alarms people who believe the present bottleneck in foreign arrivals is due to the timing of the arrivals as much as the number of passengers. Because of operating restrictions at Japan's principal overseas airport, Narita, outside Tokyo, most flights from there arrive in Honolulu during the early daylight hours. Return flights are similarly bunched in the evening. In between, the airport's present international passenger and baggage-handling facilities are little used. Spend a day in the present international terminal and you'll find that it is packed twice a day, and all but deserted the rest of the time.

A change is in the works that would eventually relieve the crowding at Honolulu. Japan is building new international airports that will lessen the dependence on Narita. Operating hours at the new facilities will be unrestricted, meaning the arrival times here will be better dispersed. No one can say whether this alone would beat today's logjams unassisted by a half-billion-dollar terminal, but it's a possibility.

Our new international terminal has been designed to eliminate the logjams of tomorrow. This assumes international activity will grow rapidly. The fickleness of international travel makes any projection almost a statement of faith. But Hawaii's political leaders and their planners are counting on an at least 33 percent rise in total visitor arrivals by the turn of the century, with most of the growth in the international category.

That's despite a number of ominous world-travel trends. One is the increased availability and use of long-range jets. The Boeing 747-400 and other new models eliminate the need for trans-Pacific passengers in either direction to stop in Hawaii. Many already bypass the islands. Airline officials believe that soon the only people coming to the state will be those intending to stay awhile.

Proponents say the airports program is a cornerstone of Hawaii's strategy for winning a major role in the Pacific Century. Bigger airports, they say, both in Honolulu and on the neighbor islands, fill a key need not only of the pivotal tourist industry but other businesses from agriculture to high tech by providing better access to worldwide markets.

"Field of Dreams." This reminds me of the movie, "Field of Dreams." For those who didn't see it, it is about an Iowa farmer who builds a baseball diamond in the middle of his corn field on the assumption that, if the diamond is there, the spirits of baseball's immortals will show up to use it.

Hawaii's politicians too seem to think supply can create its own demand. They dream of tourists showing up because the new airport is there. The rationale is reminiscent of the Hilo airport, which was expanded in the 1970s to handle swarms of mainland flights that never materialized. That airport is today grossly underutilized, a lasting monument to bad planning.

In order to service the $2 billion in debt required to finance its new airport plans, the State is having to perform a major overhaul of the airports' income sources. Revenues from the one source counted on to produce two-thirds of the airports' total annual income suddenly were chopped in half. This came as a rude surprise to state transportation officials who have done their best to play down its significance.

Big surprise. How such a thing could have happened at the beginning of the biggest capital-spending program in state history is only one of the questions that needs to be asked. Another is why it came as such a surprise. And still another is why, once the huge shortfall became known, the State proceeded with the airport program as if nothing had happened. Here's how the surprise came about.

The Airports Division of the State Department of Transportation uses airport revenues to pay for operations and service debts. Airport revenues are made up of the fees and taxes charged for the commercial use of airport facilities. Traditionally, the largest single source of the revenues has been concession fees—charges assessed by the State for giving vendors exclusive rights to do business with airport customers. Economists call it monopoly rent.

In fiscal 1991, the State's concession fees—about $275 million—amounted to 80 percent of the total airport revenues. Other revenue sources, including the landing fees and rents charged to the airlines that use the airports, were relatively minor contributors. About 84 percent of the $275 million in fees came from a single concessionaire, Duty Free Shoppers, DFS as it's now called. In 1991, DFS' $231 million in fees represented 63 percent of the airports' revenues. At least, that's the way it was budgeted. In practice, it didn't work out that way.

That same year the combination of the U.S. recession and the Persian Gulf war gave Hawaii's tourist industry its worst setback since 1949. Especially hard-hit were the businesses most dependent on Japanese visitors, who stayed home in droves. Japanese make up 90 percent of DFS' clientele, and in the early months of 1991, the retailer's duty-free sales dropped out of sight. In Hawaii, the plunge amounted to 40 percent below projections.

For 30 years, DFS has been the bulwark of airport revenues in Hawaii. Its last concession contract, for five years starting in mid-1988, was the biggest duty-free contract ever awarded in Hawaii or anywhere else: $1.15 billion in guaranteed fees over the life of the contract. The record bid was based on DFS' estimate of the growth over the next five years of its prime Japanese market, and DFS was *the* expert on this subject. It had never missed. But something went terribly wrong this time.

Practically from the start, the forecast was in trouble. Under the contract, DFS was supposed to pay the State the greater of a guaranteed annual minimum or 20 percent of sales. In the past, the percentage fee always exceeded the guarantee. But in both fiscal 1990 and 1991, the guarantee far exceeded the usual 20 percent, reaching 47 percent in

1990 and, had the full guarantee been paid, more than 60 percent of actual sales in 1991.

What went wrong. While the number of Japanese visitors continued to rise, the composition of the market was changing toward younger, budget-conscious travelers who spend far less than their predecessors on the pricey gifts that are DFS' trademark. The company should have spotted the trend before it made its billion-dollar bid for the Hawaii contract. But it didn't.

Neither did the state planners, who happily accepted DFS' expert forecasting as the basis for their ambitious airports expansion plan. DFS' $1.15 billion guarantee under the current contract was relevant but, mostly, the expansion was premised on the assumption that this was only the beginning, that DFS' revenues would continue to compound at the late 1980s rates. This "money tree" was to be used to pay for the expansion.

Although DFS surely realized by 1990 that its projections were off, it was the 1991 Persian Gulf war, helped along by the U.S. recession, that popped everybody's balloon. When the Gulf war brought a sharp drop in its Japanese business, DFS asked the airports division for relief from its guaranteed payments. The division's shocked planners had to run for their drawing boards.

DFS was permitted to defer payment of $105 million of its guaranteed fees due in 1991 until after the present contract expires on May 31, 1993. The State's airport officials really had no choice. Several admitted that to have declared DFS in default and to re-award the duty-free contract would only have hastened the day of reckoning. Any new contract would surely have guaranteed the State much lower revenues. Early in 1992, with its Japanese business recovering, at least in head count, DFS said it would be able to meet its fee schedule for the final two years of the old contract. Of course, that was a relief to state planners, but the bigger problem is that future revenues not only will not grow as projected, but likely will fall.

Less revenue. The next duty-free contract probably will not only be for a shorter term, but, more significantly, will produce only about half the revenues envisioned by the current contract.

Prior to this debacle, concession fees, led by DFS, made life easy not only for the State but for others who did business at the airports. The

huge concession revenues sheltered them by enabling lower than normal rents, landing fees and other airport payments. In effect, it was a giveaway. But nobody saw it that way. Airport authorities were interested only in covering their operating and financing costs. And the airport users, like business people everywhere, were interested in saving money.

In the future, the State wants to replace the present use-charge schedule based on the facilities' "market" value with one based on actual costs. The aim would be to cover the airports' operating costs, whatever they are.

But the airlines are skeptical. They are looking at enormous increases in their airport costs per passenger. The State's own estimate is for these costs to zoom from 69 cents in 1991 to $8.18 in 1995.

The airlines will pass the increase on to passengers, who may not notice another $8 tacked on their airfares. But, the $8 figure assumes passenger numbers will continue to grow. If they don't, the charge will have to be higher, perhaps much higher. Ironically, the airport expansion could increase costs to the point that even more flights get routed over, rather than through Hawaii.

The airports expansion is a perfect example of what economists call "revenue driven" spending. Only in this case, the revenue may have been a mirage. State officials, meanwhile, are off in a corner assuring each other, "if we build it, they will come."

"WHO GETS THE CHECK?....UH, WHERE'S EVERYBODY??...."

CHAPTER 35

FUNDING RAPID TRANSIT

LOUIS A. ROSE
Professor of Economics
University of Hawaii

"Assuming Oahu gets fixed rail, is there some 'fair' way to help pay for it?"

As of mid-1992, the fixed-rail tab was to be paid with excise and income taxes. Because landowners in the vicinity of the planned transit stations are going to get "windfalls" as the value of their land increases dramatically, it makes sense to consider a special tax on them. After all, why should they get rich at taxpayer expense?

Whenever there are public projects, there are windfall gains (or losses) to nearby landowners. Allowing risk-bearing investors to keep such gains is as American as apple pie.

On the other hand, there is another American tradition of special assessments to pay for sidewalks and storm drains in old neighborhoods. By installing these, the government increases the value of nearby properties. Costs generally are paid by issuing bonds, but payments on the principal and interest are at least partly covered by special annual taxes against the benefiting properties. The only properties taxed are those in a special assessment district abutting the sidewalks or in the storm-drain-catchment neighborhood.

Special assessment. The Honolulu City & County administration should seriously consider a special assessment on properties near transit stops at least to help cover the operating deficit. This revenue source also could be tapped to pay for capital-cost overruns. There are at least two arguments that the benefiting properties should be taxed.

First, you should pay for what you get from the government, just as you pay for what you get at the market. Widely accepted, this is called the "benefit principle" of taxation. We use it, for example, to rationalize taxes at the gas pump. Those revenues are used for road construction and maintenance, thereby ensuring that drivers pay for the benefits of government-provided roads.

Second, if land value increments (minus inflation) are unearned by their owners, this "profit" should be taxed away. When a transit station is constructed, the owners of nearby properties do nothing productive to increase the value. Rather, the value derives from a government decision on behalf of the public, and so it should be captured for the public. This argument, popularized by economist Henry George, is appealing because it is a tax that does not discourage productive activity.

Would it be fair? Before we accept the notion that the assessment is fair, we ought to consider that practically everything government does raises (or lowers) the value of someone's land. Should a golf course development permit, construction of a pumping station, and widening of Kalanianaole Highway all trigger assessments on property whose land values rise? The revenue could be used to pay for these projects or even to compensate those whose land values fall. In principle, this is attractive. In practice, the costs of administering assessments on all but the largest projects (such as, perhaps, major transit stations), probably make it not worthwhile.

If we accept the notion that a tax is fair and administratively feasible for transit stations, then how would such a tax work? One possibility is the city would define district bounds (perhaps out to a half mile walking distance) around each station. The tax should be on land only; if it were also on capital improvements, that would discourage high density development near the stations, right where we want it. The tax would be collected annually.

Two variants of this tax should be considered. The first is ideal and the second is practical. The base of the first tax is 50 percent of the land value increment due to station access. The amount of the tax on a parcel would be the product of a 50 percent tax rate multiplied by the difference between parcel value when the station location was first announced and parcel value following initial operation. The increment, and the rate as well, could be revised periodically following initial station operation. (The increment would be adjusted downward by the amount of community-wide land appreciation during the ever-lengthening period of measurement.)

What would be the capital value of this tax liability on a typical parcel of land? It would vary from one parcel to the next. Parcels close to the station would pay higher taxes than those more distant. Some parcels within a district would not necessarily increase in value; they would not be taxed. To illustrate a possible case, suppose the value of a parcel was initially $1 million and that its adjusted value in the absence of the tax would be $2 million. It can be shown that legislation of this tax would create a capitalized tax liability of roughly $500,000. This would depress the parcel's value from $2 million down to only $1.5 million.

How much of the transit system's operating deficit would be covered by such tax revenues? The answer requires some forecasting of the sizes of the deficit and of revenue collections. The forecast of revenue collections at any specified tax rate will be more uncertain than are revenues from the ordinary property tax. If the revenues actually collected are short of the forecast, then public officials will have to scramble to obtain additional revenues from alternative sources.

Others benefit, too. Even if it were possible to pay for all of this deficit out of special assessment revenues, it would not necessarily be fair to do so. That is because the benefit principle holds that costs should be borne in proportion to benefits, and property owners in the neighborhood may not be the only beneficiaries. If, as some advocates of the transit system allege, the freeways will be less clogged, it follows that drivers should also pay some of the deficit.

The only experience with special assessments based on changes in property value occurred in London between 1895 and 1902. Five projects—bridges and their approaches and road widenings—were

CONGA LINE

specially assessed. This approach to financing public transportation was abandoned, partly because of opposition of taxable property owners and partly because the revenues raised were not worth the cost of assessment and arbitrating appeals.

The cost of administering benefit assessment district taxation in Honolulu should be a major concern in determining whether this whole idea is feasible. The specification of districts around stations, and the assessment of land value increments attributable solely to station access (after deflating for citywide land inflation) will be difficult, and will raise objections by property owners in those districts. The potential furor may make it difficult for some public officials to endorse such a tax. And the costs of resolving property owners' objections through the appeals process could make the tax wasteful.

An alternative type of tax would be more practical to administer, and more likely to be enacted. In 1983 the State of California passed a law enabling transit authorities to set up benefit assessment districts, and in 1985 such districts were created on a major segment of Los Angeles County's proposed transit system. The tax revenues are to be used to help pay the construction costs.

The Los Angeles tax, to be collected annually, is simply $.30 per square foot times the land area or improvement area, whichever is larger. It would be possible for us to increase the tax rate and apply it to the land area alone, so as not to discourage property improvements.

This tax is not as fair as the previously described tax which is proportional to station-induced increases in land value. On the other hand, it is simpler to administer, and the revenues should be easier to forecast.

In short, tapping some of the property owners' windfall gains that result from the new stations is a good idea on fairness grounds. We just have to be sure that the revenue source is dependable and the costs of administering the tax are not too high. Although somewhat flawed on fairness grounds, an assessment per square foot against land may be the most practical way to capture a part of the land value increment.

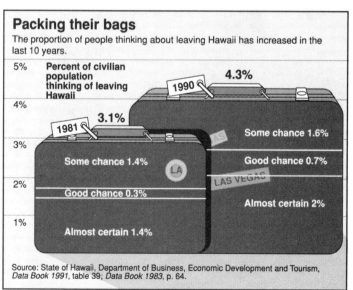

Packing their bags

The proportion of people thinking about leaving Hawaii has increased in the last 10 years.

Percent of civilian population thinking of leaving Hawaii

1981 — 3.1%
- Some chance 1.4%
- Good chance 0.3%
- Almost certain 1.4%

1990 — 4.3%
- Some chance 1.6%
- Good chance 0.7%
- Almost certain 2%

Source: State of Hawaii, Department of Business, Economic Development and Tourism, *Data Book 1991*, table 39; *Data Book 1983*, p. 64.

CHAPTER 36

OUT MIGRATION

WALTER MIKLIUS
Professor of Economics and Agricultural Economics
University of Hawaii

"If Hawaii is paradise, why do so many people leave?"

How many people actually leave Hawaii each year? I called Bob Schmitt, the recently retired state statistician, who knows just about everything about Hawaii. He told me that no one really knows. I also called Bob Gardner at the East-West Center's Program on Population. He's the resident *guru* when it comes to Hawaii's population. It turned out that he, too, didn't know. The data simply do not exist.

As long as no one knows for sure how many people move from Hawaii each year, I thought I'd try to make an educated guess. To do so, I looked at a survey conducted by the State Department of Health that asks lots of nosey questions, including how likely it is that the respondent will be living some place other than Hawaii one year hence. Those who indicated on the most recent survey that they might leave Hawaii were distributed as follows:

- Some possibility of living elsewhere   18,344
- A good chance of living elsewhere   6,954
- Almost certain to be living elsewhere   15,197

Of course, we have no idea whether these people actually moved. But to estimate how many of them moved, I assumed a 25 percent probability that the respondents in the first group moved (that's a pretty small probability); 50 percent probability for the second group; and 90 percent probability for the third group. The math worked out to 21,740 people, close to 2 percent of Hawaii's total population.

Real estate developer Stuart T.K. Ho (at exactly the same time, but unbeknownst to me) tried to answer the same question by analyzing driver's license data from California, Washington, Oregon and Nevada. Basically, he multiplied the number of Hawaii licenses surrendered in these four states in 1990 by 150 percent (total population divided by the number old enough to get a driver's license), and then subtracted 40 percent of the estimated number of military and dependents moving from Hawaii that year (no one keeps track of where they all go, and an assumption that 40 percent go to these four states sounds reasonable to me). The resulting number (10,865) was almost exactly 1 percent of the 1990 Hawaii population. If we assume that, say, 50 percent moved to one of the other 45 states or the District of Columbia, we end up real close to the same 2 percent figure I arrived at.

For 2 percent of a civilian population to move annually from any place, much less a place like Hawaii where the costs of moving are especially high, is noteworthy.

Classic study. Why would all of these people leave? A classic 1956 study concluded that residents of any community sufficiently dissatisfied with the taxes they have to pay or the quality of public services they receive will "vote with their feet" (move) to states with lower taxes or better public services. High taxes undoubtedly play a part in decisions to leave Hawaii. It is hardly a coincidence that a substantial number move to Nevada, a state with low taxes on residents. However, it is unlikely that taxes are the principal reason why people leave Hawaii.

Moving from one place to another place is never easy. And the total cost of moving from Hawaii is much higher than of moving from one place to another place on the Mainland. That big ocean separating Hawaii from every place else magnifies the emotional and psychological pain, as well as the financial cost. For this reason, I doubt that high taxes or poor government services were important enough reasons for the majority of these people to warrant moving from Hawaii.

The likelihood of a move is much higher at certain times in life. One such time is when a person graduates from high school and goes to a mainland college. This student is much more likely to stay on the Mainland because he or she already has paid part of the costs of moving. (Again, the costs are emotional and psychological as well as financial.) Consequently, it is likely that a significant portion of the 2 percent moving from Hawaii each year are at this early stage of adult life.

Hawaii's brain drain. It is widely believed that Hawaii's best and brightest students go to college or postgraduate school on the Mainland. If this is true (and I believe it is), Hawaii may very well have a brain drain problem like that commonly found in third-world countries.

The decision not to return to Hawaii is reinforced by the lack of demand for skilled labor here. Our local economy is dominated by low-wage service industries—primarily tourism—that employ mostly unskilled labor. Skilled people, such as engineers, typically must leave Hawaii to find financially rewarding jobs. Stated another way, Hawaii's lack of diversification means many young people cannot find jobs in Hawaii that match their skills or aspirations.

No one, to my knowledge, has really looked at the size of the brain drain. So I called Punahou School and asked for information on what happened to its 1981 graduating class. Eleven years is certainly long enough for virtually everyone in the class to have finished school. Of the 422 students who graduated from Punahou that year, 78 percent (328) went to mainland colleges, 15 percent (65) attended college in Hawaii, and the post-secondary education actions of the remaining 7 percent (29) were unknown. Of those who went to the Mainland, 53 percent (175) settled there. Of the 65 graduates who stayed in Hawaii to study, 25 percent (16) later moved away.

It would be interesting to contrast Punahou's record with similar statistics for a public high school. I called the principals of several to get similar data, but learned they don't have such records.

My guess is that Punahou graduates have a much higher propensity to leave Hawaii and, once having left, are much less likely to return. Punahou is not the only excellent private school in Hawaii, and its experiences probably parallel those of other first-rate schools.

However, the questioner probably isn't talking about the outflow of talented young people from Hawaii. That has been going on for years.

What's been receiving a lot of publicity recently is the out-migration of nonstudents. My own observation is that the propensity to leave Hawaii is particularly high among retirees. This may surprise some since many retirees own their home and therefore are not directly affected by the high cost of housing. Plus, a touted advantage of retiring here is that Hawaii doesn't tax retirement income.

The propensity for people to leave Hawaii upon retirement can be explained partly by the fact that retirement is another point in one's life when relocation costs are low. There is no job to leave, and children may have already moved to the Mainland. Moreover, Hawaii's high cost of living is an inducement to leave. People on lower retirement incomes quickly realize that their dollars stretch farther on the Mainland.

Cashing in. A major factor in the decision to move often is the high cost of housing in Hawaii, even for retirees who own their homes and already have paid off the mortgage. Why would these people have reason to sell? The answer is simple: You can stay in your small home in Hawaii and have little cash, or you can live in a nicer home elsewhere and have extra cash for travel, hobbies, loans to the kids, etc.

In short, at that stage of life it makes a lot of sense to sell the Hawaii house, buy or rent a cheaper place on the Mainland, and enjoy a better balance between what you "spend" on housing and what you spend on everything else.

So, does Hawaii's out-migration consist primarily of college-bound kids and soon-to-be retirees like me? Several years ago I would have answered "yes," but that has changed.

Sky-high living costs (including record highs in real estate) and relatively unattractive job opportunities have combined to cause many "in-betweeners," who otherwise love Hawaii, to move despite the high costs of doing so. As the following "Letter to the Editor" indicates, at least some are happy with their decision. Those of you who remain better think through the social implications of having 2 percent of an entire civilian population move out each year (even if it is more than replaced by natural increase and in-migration). What's propelling that 2 percent had better get proper attention before it's too late.

Aloha nui loa, and will the last kamaaina out please turn out the lights?

Their paradise is not in Hawaii

We have waited for six months to write this letter, waiting to see if our feelings would change, they haven't. If anything they have been reinforced by "Hawaiian egotism," the belief that "Hawaii no ka oi!"

My husband, a Molokai-born Hawaiian and myself, a "haole" spending half my life in Hawaii, were part of the "great white flight" this spring. We left behind our children, brothers, sisters and wonderful friends in order to find a better quality of life and thankfully we found it.

We now own a wonderful "affordable" home that by Hawaii standards would be unaffordable. Our grocery bill has been reduced by one-third (would you believe, $1.50 a gallon for milk ... no wonder Maurice Sullivan has such fabulous houses). We can jump in our car and be in the mountains or at the beach in less time than it takes to go from Kahala to Hawaii Kai rush hour! And there are plenty of fine restaurants to get the "exotic" foods we are used to.

Our only regret—we didn't make our move to the mainland sooner. We have found that most transplanted Hawaiians feel the same way and there are lots of us up here.

The people here practice the "aloha spirit" daily from giving helpful advice on how to winterize our pool, to where to get good "seasoned firewood," to the best wineries to visit and great customer service is top priority at most businesses.

Don't get us wrong, we do miss our friends and family, the balmy breezes, swaying palms and blue ocean, Joe Moore and Longs, but it is a relief to not have to deal with round-the-clock traffic, politicians with questionable regard for their constituents and the cost of living that requires most people to work two jobs to barely make ends meet.

We just want other people to know that there is life outside Hawaii ... the good life!

[Letters to the Editor, *Honolulu Star-Bulletin,* 10/29/91]

CHAPTER 37

WELFARE

EDWIN T. FUJII
Professor of Economics
University of Hawaii

"Is the level of welfare benefits in Hawaii adequate, inadequate, or overly generous?"

That question really doesn't have a "correct" answer. Certainly it is possible to find informed opinions, as well as uninformed opinions. Let me tell you a bit about Hawaii's welfare system so your opinion can be "informed."

Assistance generally can be divided into two categories: cash grants and noncash benefits. Both are funded and administered jointly by the state and federal governments. People cannot own much if they want to qualify for either type. Maximum assets in Hawaii for a family of four, for example, are $1,000 to qualify for cash grants, $3,500 for medical assistance, and $2,000 for food stamps. People can qualify for welfare even if they have an income, and there is no stated maximum. However, welfare benefits are reduced by a predetermined "cutback" rate. Consequently, anyone with an income that approaches whatever the poverty line happens to be at that time, generally will not qualify for any benefits. They will have been "cut back" to zero.

As of July 1991, "poverty lines" were:

Size of Family	Annual Income
Single person	$7,608
Family of 2	10,200
Family of 3	12,804
Family of 4	15,408
Family of 5	18,000
Family of 6	20,604

Qualifying for grants. To qualify for a cash-grant program people must be more than just poor; they must also fit into well-defined categories. For example, those who are both poor and blind, disabled or aged are eligible for Supplemental Security Income. Those who are poor and have children, may qualify for Aid to Families with Dependent Children (AFDC). Most AFDC recipients are families without a male parent. However, a small AFDC-UP (unemployed parent) program provides assistance for intact families who can demonstrate deprivation in the absence of aid. Another cash grant program, called general assistance, aids a small number of poor people who do not fit into either of the above categories.

Noncash assistance programs such as food stamps and Medicaid were developed in part because of a concern that cash benefits might be spent unwisely or, worse yet, on destructive agents such as liquor and drugs, thus depriving the children of recipients. Noncash grant programs are attractive in that they are limited to food, housing and medical care—goods that address basic needs and are likely to directly benefit the applicant's children as well.

In January 1992, a record 25 million Americans, or nearly 1 in 10, received food-stamp aid. Despite Hawaii's long-time low unemployment rate, 1 in 12 here were receiving food stamps in Hawaii that same month.

The welfare system is a "patchwork" affair, in part because of conflicting concerns. Most people genuinely desire to assist the truly needy. This instinct, however, is tempered by an unwillingness to aid

THE PRICE OF PARADISE

able-bodied adults. Also of great concern (especially now that many mainland states are reducing their benefit levels) is the possibility that qualifying individuals will migrate to Hawaii in part because we have been identified as the fifth most generous state when it comes to welfare. California, although poised to reduce its benefits, was two notches up in third place at the time of the survey.

Hawaii's welfare system is such that, in theory, all people will be caught by a safety net at or above the poverty line. In reality, some potential recipients either don't know about all the possible benefits or are intimidated by the bureaucratic application process.

Representative payments for cash and noncash programs are listed below. These numbers were computed by the State Department of Human Services (DHS) for a hypothetical family of four in 1990 and are the most recent data available.

Cash Grants (covering basics and shelter)	$9,120
Food Stamp Benefits	$4,008
Estimated Medical Benefits (actually may be higher or lower)	$2,354
Total Welfare Benefits	$15,482
1990 Poverty Line (family of 4)	$14,604
Total Welfare Benefits÷Poverty Line	1.06

While tax-free income of $15,482 for a family of four may seem generous, especially when measured against the poverty line, few readers could credibly argue that these benefits could provide a comfortable lifestyle in Hawaii.

Once eligible, families that receive aid find it difficult to wean themselves from it. For example, after some exemptions, grants are reduced dollar for dollar with respect to every additional dollar earned. How enthusiastic would you be about finding and holding a job at, say, $6 an hour if every single penny effectively had to be paid back to DHS in the form of a smaller benefit check? Under these circumstances it's a wonder any recipients are gainfully employed.

While other grant programs reduce aid more gradually (the "cutback" rate is 25 percent for food stamps, for example), when the various welfare programs are tiered, a family that works to get itself off welfare may find working harder only *lowers* its standard of living.

AFDC also provides disincentives for the formation of families and incentives for the dissolution of intact families. Consider the plight of a pregnant teenager. Should she form a household with the father of that child, their financial outlook might be bleak. In Hawaii in 1990, almost two-thirds of the graduates of the high school class of 1989 were earning less than $6 an hour. High-school dropouts face an even less attractive labor market. If the father worked full time (40 hours a week), 50 weeks (2,000 hours a year), the family would still fall below the poverty line. If the mother goes it alone, however, she can qualify for benefits that probably lift her to or above the poverty line, and the father can pocket all his earnings.

Similarly, consider the plight of a chronically unemployed male head of a low-income household. The message is clear. His family would be financially better off if he abandoned it.

Inadequate data. How long do people stay on welfare? Unfortunately, DHS does not keep such statistics.

It might also prove interesting to calculate how much of the money going into the welfare system actually ends up in the hands of the needy. Cynics have called welfare a full-employment program for its many administrators and social workers. Unfortunately, the raw data for Hawaii are not available and interpreting it would be tricky anyway. For example, it would be quite difficult to divide the budget into administrative overhead, welfare benefits, and other truly essential social services provided by DHS.

Hawaii, like its nearest neighbor California, has been a generous state. Southern states such as Texas, Louisiana and Mississippi provide less than a third as much aid. Under the U.S. Constitution, all citizens, rich and poor alike, are free to migrate. This includes the right to move to Hawaii in search of more generous aid. State welfare residency requirements are consistently struck down by the federal courts. In a worst case scenario, welfare migration could bankrupt our limited resources.

A recent local rumor claims an unidentified mainland jurisdiction has a simple and relatively inexpensive way of dealing with its homeless—it gives them one-way tickets to Hawaii. This supposedly is described there as a win-win solution. The mainland jurisdiction is permanently relieved of its financial responsibility and the homeless person's income is tripled by moving to paradise. These stories have been investigated thoroughly by DHS which has a strong incentive to determine the facts. As of the spring of 1992, it had found absolutely no evidence that the stories are true. Let's all hope this is just someone's bad joke.

Depends on values. Some people believe the first principle of welfare should be to make life so uncomfortable for recipients that they will have a burning desire to get off welfare. Others speak of things like human dignity, argue that every citizen has a right to more than just basic existence and "there but for the grace of God ...." And, of course, most people soften when children are involved. No one wants them to suffer. Values come into play.

The founder of Habilitat—a Windward Oahu drug-rehabilitation center "that teaches residents to break drug dependency through discipline and self-respect"—in the spring of 1992 offered to house and train 50 homeless adults for one year without charge. According to the press, no one took him up on his offer despite his promise to have them ready to be productive citizens within a year. Stories like this, whether true or exaggerated, harden the hearts of taxpayers and work to the disadvantage of welfare recipients who are truly deserving.

Stronger incentives to work could be accomplished if only benefits declined less as earned income increased. Recipients who find themselves financially better off by working harder likely will do so. However, a lower "cutback" rate on earned income means that more earners would be eligible for aid, thus imposing a larger burden on taxpayers. Lowering the basic grant could cut the tax burden, but at the cost of lowering the quality of life for those most in need. There are no easy answers.

Our choices thus far have been relatively easy due to the longstanding healthy Hawaiian economy, which as of early 1992 had weathered the 1991-92 U.S. recession with a remarkably low unemployment rate of about 3 percent. Hawaii's economy, however, is inextricably linked with the national economy. With the slow rate of productivity growth and the resultant slow growth in real incomes in the nation as a whole, the Hawaiian economy may yet sputter and stall.

According to a *New York Times*—CBS News 1992 poll, 44 percent of Americans said they were no longer bothered by the presence of homeless people. Michigan, for example, confronted with budget deficits in large part related to layoffs in the auto industry, cut off all general assistance to able-bodied adults in 1991 just as the winter snow began to fall.

Charity comes easily in a robust economy. How we deal with the poor during hard times tests the depth and resiliency of our vaunted aloha spirit.

EVERYBODY FAVORS 'HOMELESS VILLAGES' AND WHERE TO PUT THEM...

Homework

CHAPTER 38

HAWAII'S FUTURE

A.A. "BUD" SMYSER
Contributing Editor
Honolulu Star-Bulletin

"What lies ahead for the people of Hawaii?"

State and local governments will be far more important to Hawaii in the future than they are now. Attracting talented community-minded people to government will be crucial. I feel strongly about this.

Basic concerns. First, consider our wants. We want a Hawaii that preserves its aloha spirit of friendliness, sharing and love for the land. We want to protect and enhance our environment, to offer jobs, first-rate health care and education to all, to put a roof over everyone's head, and to treat our disadvantaged residents with compassion.

Second, consider what is happening to the ownership of Hawaii. More and more of it is owned "offshore," less and less by people who have the commitment that grows from knowing their children and grandchildren will grow up here.

Absentee ownership is not of itself bad. Outside capital has been basic to our growth, wealth and ever-increasing variety of choice. But future-shaping decisions made from afar may not always put Hawaii's best long-term interests first. To assure that these decisions are of our people, by our people and for our people, we will have to look more to our elected state and local governments.

Importance and role of government. I say this with something of a shudder. Government can let us down, too. That's why I stress the importance of attracting talented, community-minded people to it.

Government should encourage businesses that put in more than they take out, and that respect the above goals. Fortunately, we already have many good citizen businesses, some of them absentee-owned.

Conversely, government should discourage buccaneers and exploiters who lack respect for the general welfare.

This does not require bigger government, just better government. Government should set the rules of the game, but be less of a player than it is now. It is too big already. The collapse of socialism shows that government is no good at running economies. Might it not be equally bad at performing other services? The more services we can turn over to market-oriented private enterprises that play within the rules, the better.

Hawaii has some of the best and most affordable health care in America with a system based on private enterprise. We should carry this lesson into housing, schools of choice and numerous other services that could be leaner and more effective if privately run. We can do it if leaders emerge to articulate such goals. As voters we must scrutinize ever more closely those who want to help run our government, then choose the best. This becomes more important every day.

So how do we attract more talented, community-minded people to government? I'm not sure, but I have a few ideas.

More debates, less sign waving. Keep legislative and county council service part-time. That way we have a bigger talent pool to draw on. Let's not fear the legislator who goes back to a private job or megabucks business, or to a union to call a strike, maybe even against government. Let's trust the concept of representative government to see that these talented people contend in an open forum so that their best ideas can be exposed to and weighed by their colleagues and the public. Campaign debates are tough on candidates. They are especially risky for incumbents because they give exposure to lesser known rivals. However, they offer valuable insights into both issues and leadership qualities. We, the people, should demand more of them and less of simple, safe techniques like sign waving.

Constructive attitude. My colleagues in the media should have more faith. We should report more of the good instead of pouncing mostly on the bad. But the public must support this by showing its interest in the good as well as the bad. I don't demean calls for more investigative reporting. We have a lot and more would be fine. But let's be specific in our criticisms and not demean all politics as "dirty." A key role of politics is to bring us together, sometimes across wide differences. It is a high art.

Expand horizons. One much-criticized perk of top-level government service is travel. We in the media tend to call trips "junkets". Our leaders need travel to broaden their knowledge and perspectives. By extending horizons such travel can be a good investment for us. It also can be an attraction to public service. However, we should peek over the shoulders of our travelers to see that they really work at their missions, thereby earning the right to a little play as well.

The 1992 legislative flap over first-class and personal-interest travel helped develop clearer rules. It also showed there is no generalized public resistance to travel if the purpose is deemed worthy. Both are pluses. A third plus might be to send media representatives along on more missions. They need broadening, too, and they could play a useful watchdog role.

Elect leaders, not followers. Yes, we want ethical conduct. But let's not distrust our public servants to the point of making public service unattractive to people who can lead. Reasonable disclosure of private interests and open decision making should be our main emphasis.

Election from large multimember districts should be more widely employed. Small single-member districts provoke greater demand on incumbents for narrow-gauge spending and narrow-gauge thinking on area-wide concerns.

Appreciate business. It may surprise some to learn that most businesses do give back more than they take out. At a minimum they create jobs and pay taxes. Most do more.

The best of them are good corporate citizens. They volunteer money and personnel time to community causes. They protect the environment. They show social concern for their employees. They profit by filling a need. They reinvest big portions of their profits back so their business will grow for the future.

We would be in terrible shape without them. There are the "bad

Past

Future?

guys," of course. Government can discourage them, setting standards to which they must conform in order to continue doing business in Hawaii.

Happy companies with happy employees are more the rule than the exception in Hawaii.

Important step. Do I really think we can shrink the size of government in the future? I do. I do. Read what other contributors to this book say about privatization. It's a trend nationwide. Governments are contracting out the management of hospitals, traffic control, highway maintenance, refuse collection, jails, even some police and fire services. In most of these cases governments are getting more bang for their buck.

All too often bureaucrats fight to have more people under them because that's the road to higher pay classification. Turf battles ensue. For fear of being diminished they resist transferring underlings to more efficient employment in another branch. They fight for new positions, rarely recommend abolishing any. A lot of time and paperwork are wasted on these battles. Pretty soon branches of government have employees who must spend most of their time in committee meetings finding out what the others are doing. Many government employees have more incentive to protect themselves by never waiving a rule than to see that things get accomplished.

Private management has more flexibility to streamline its work force and reward employees for results rather than how many workers are under them.

We also should diminish government's regulatory role. It is ludicrous and cost-raising that we take about seven years to approve a new housing development because of the overlapping regulatory agencies involved. To break this regulatory grip will be to diminish the power of politicians and regulators. It won't be easy. But it must be done.

Political leadership. Occasionally I am asked what I think of present political leadership in Hawaii. I wish there were more of it— leadership, that is. I don't see enough leaders expressing clear visions for the future and winning others to rally round.

The pace of life is quickening due to computers, fax machines and other technological advances. The scope of our interest is broadening because of global television and communications. Our personal prob-

lems are becoming more complicated, partly because of urbanization. Instead of working out problems with our neighbors we turn more and more to legislators, government administrators and the courts to solve them for us. We are burying these people with workload and they are burying us with bureaucracy.

More and more we need leadership to help us cope—people who can meld the goals of all of us toward improving the common good. I mean true leaders, not demagogues who pander to lowest common denominators. Right now, both in Hawaii and nationally, we need strong leaders to identify workable ways to improve the lot of our troubled underclasses and rally support to implement effective programs. This is an area of uncertainty. But we start with the certainty that most of the old ways haven't worked.

Favorite examples. I have two favorite examples of the kind of leadership I mean. One was a Democrat. One was a Republican. Their philosophies differed. But each worked for the common good as he saw it. Each stated clear goals. What you saw was pretty much what you got. When they suffered political defeat—and both did—they didn't say: "Back to the drawing boards. I'll change my program to something more popular."

Instead they were inner-directed people with strong beliefs. Each must have said: "I lost, but I'm right. I won't change with the wind." The voters finally came around to them. They elected John A. Burns to be Governor of Hawaii and Ronald Reagan as President of the United States. You may agree or disagree with these men and their records. Reagan remains controversial. Even though he correctly called the U.S.S.R. an "evil empire," helped speed its dissolution and presided over a period of peace and prosperity, the pluses and minuses of his administration are still being evaluated. Whatever the final verdict, his agenda was clear and he was dedicated to doing the best for America as he saw it. I would welcome more leaders like both Ronald Reagan and John Burns. A debate between the two would have been in the best democratic tradition.

Dick Adair
Editorial Cartoonist
The *Honolulu Advertiser*

Winner of numerous local and national awards including the Freedoms Foundation Medal and Honor Certificate and first place 1988 "Best of the West" for editorial cartooning; author and illustrator of best-selling children's books, *The Story of Aloha Bear* and *Aloha Bear and the Meaning of Aloha*; his works have appeared in *New York Times*, *Newsweek*, *Readers' Digest* and *The Washington Post*.

Corky Trinidad
Political Cartoonist
Honolulu Star-Bulletin

Award-winning, nationally syndicated political cartoonist with the *Honolulu Star-Bulletin* since 1969; first cartoonist of Asian descent to break into the American cartoon journalism field; his works have appeared in newspapers nationally, including *The Washington Post, New York Times, Los Angeles Times, Miami Herald,* and *Philadelphia Inquirer,* as well as *Time* and *Newsweek* magazines.

AUTHORS' BIOGRAPHICAL SKETCHES

Paul H. Brewbaker
Economist
Bank of Hawaii

Lectured in economics at the University of Wisconsin, the University of Hawaii and Hawaii Pacific University; past president and director of the Hawaii Economic Association; member of the Council on Revenues, the Hawaii Visitor's Bureau Market Research Committee, and the Honolulu Board of Realtor's Research Roundtable.

David L. Callies
Professor of Law
William S. Richardson School of Law
University of Hawaii

Author of *Regulating Paradise: Land Use Controls in Hawaii*; past chairman, section on State & Local Government Law, American Bar Association; member, American Law Institute and American Institute of Certified Planners; member and past president, Aloha Chapter, Lambda Alpha, an international land economics society.

John P. Dolly
Dean and Professor of Education
College of Education
University of Hawaii

Dean and Professor of Education at the University of Hawaii at Manoa since 1986; Dean of Education, University of Wyoming 1981-1986, and department chair and assistant dean at the University of South Carolina, 1975-1981.

Robert Ebel
Director, State Fiscal Services
Policy Economic Group
KPMG Peat Marwick Main & Co.
Washington, D.C.

Directs state fiscal research for KPMG Peat Marwick's Policy Economics Group; formerly finance manager, U.S. Advisory Commission on Intergovernmental Relations; directed fiscal studies for Guam, Minnesota, and Nevada; economics columnist for The *Honolulu Advertiser* and the *St. Paul Pioneer Press*.

Thomas M. Foley, Esq.
Foley Maehara Judge Nip & Chang

Tax attorney active in tax litigation, including real-property tax appeals; former member of Hawaii State Tax Review Commission; member of Tax Foundation of Hawaii and of Historic Hawaii Foundation Executive Committee; current president of Downtown Improvement Association.

William F. Fox
Professor of Economics
University of Tennessee

Recently served as Visiting Professor of Economics at the University of Hawaii at Manoa; was a consultant for the Hawaii State Tax Review Commission; has published numerous articles in the areas of taxation and economic development; consulting work includes analyzing public policy issues for six states and eight countries.

Edwin T. Fujii
Professor of Economics
University of Hawaii

B.A. with highest honors in economics from the University of Hawaii in 1968 and Ph.D. in economics from Stanford University in 1973; published extensively and taught graduate and undergraduate courses in labor economics, public finance and urban economics.

Robert W. Gardner
Research Associate, Program on Population
East-West Center

Ph.D. in demography, University of California at Berkeley; at the East-West Center for 21 years, currently Research Associate and Assistant Director for Graduate Study at the Program on Population; publications include *The Demographic Situation in Hawaii* and *Life Tables by Ethnic Group for Hawaii*.

Christopher Grandy
Visiting Assistant Professor of Economics
University of Hawaii

Ph.D. in economics, University of California at Berkeley; Assistant Professor of Economics, Barnard College, Columbia University; visiting professor at University of Hawaii in 1992; author of forthcoming *New Jersey and the Fiscal Origins of Modern American Corporation Law*.

Lowell L. Kalapa
President
Tax Foundation of Hawaii

B.A. and M.A. degrees in journalism from the Medill School of Journalism, Northwestern University; as president of the nonprofit research group, Tax Foundation of Hawaii, he works with elected officials, community groups and the public at large in bringing about a better understanding of state and local government finances.

L. Dew Kaneshiro
Gender and Other Fairness Project Coordinator
Hawaii State Judiciary

Attorney and project coordinator for the Hawaii Supreme Court's Committee on Gender and Other Fairness; undergraduate degree, San Francisco State University; J.D., New York University School of Law; practiced law on the East Coast, specializing in First Amendment, privacy rights, and commercial litigation.

H.K. Bruss Keppeler, Esq.
Lyons Brandt Cook & Hiramatsu

Attorney in private practice concentrating in real estate, corporate and estate-planning law; B.A. (Public Administration) and J.D., University of Washington; of Hawaiian ancestry and a student of Hawaiian history, he advocates preservation of Hawaiian culture and the betterment of conditions for Hawaiians.

Professor Sumner J. La Croix
Professor of Economics
University of Hawaii

Professor of Economics at the University of Hawaii at Manoa; received B.A. in mathematics from the University of Virginia in 1976, Ph.D., University of Washington in 1981; research focuses on the development of property rights in land, natural resources and intellectual property in Asia and the Pacific.

Leroy O. Laney
Vice President and Chief Economist
First Hawaiian Bank

First Hawaiian Bank's Chief Economist since 1990; Ph.D. in economics, University of Colorado; MBA, Emory University; engineering undergraduate degree from Georgia Tech; served in the Federal Reserve System, the U.S. Treasury and the President's Council of Economic Advisers, as well as academia.

James Mak
Professor of Economics
University of Hawaii

Ph.D. in economics, Purdue University; leading authority on the economics of the tourist industry; published extensively in the area of tourism; editorial board of the *Journal of Travel Research*; widely recognized for research on Hawaii's economy.

George Mason
Editorial Page Editor and Publisher Emeritus
Pacific Business News

Founded Crossroads Press, Inc. in 1963 to publish *Pacific Business News* after seven-and-a-half years as Territorial and State Director of Economic Development; numerous leadership positions in nonprofit organizations in Hawaii, including chairman of the Chamber of Commerce of Hawaii, Better Business Bureau and Junior Achievement.

Coralie Chun Matayoshi, Esq.
Executive Director
Hawaii State Bar Association

Graduate of University of California at Berkeley and Hastings Law School; former trial attorney for the U.S. Department of Justice, Antitrust Division in Washington, D.C.; private law practice; executive director of the Hawaii Institute for Continuing Legal Education; and past president of the Hawaii State Bar Association Young Lawyers Division.

David McClain
Henry A. Walker, Jr. Distinguished Professor
  of Business Enterprise and Financial Economics & Institutions
College of Business Administration
University of Hawaii

Ph.D. in economics, M.I.T.; taught at M.I.T., Boston University and Keio University, Tokyo; senior staff economist on the Council of Economic Advisers under President Jimmy Carter; frequent consultant to business; contributor to national financial electronic and print-news media; author of *Apocalypse on Wall Street*.

Walter Miklius
Professor of Economics and Agricultural Economics
University of Hawaii

> Ph.D. in economics, University of California at Los Angeles; taught at University of California at Davis; economist with U.S. Department of Agriculture in Washington, D.C.; joined University of Hawaii faculty in 1967.

James E.T. Moncur
Professor of Economics
University of Hawaii

> Professor of Economics and researcher at the Water Resources Research Center, University of Hawaii since 1969; published on the pricing of water, drought management, the value of water, conservation and the connection between water law and economics.

Bruce S. Plasch
President
Decision Analysts Hawaii, Inc.

> Ph.D. in engineering-economic systems, Stanford University; economic and financial consultant in Hawaii since 1971; president of Decision Analysts Hawaii, a firm specializing in economic development, public policy analysis, land and housing economics, market assessments, project feasibility, valuations and economic impact analysis.

Louis A. Rose
Professor of Economics
University of Hawaii

> Has taught applied microeconomics and researched land and housing economics, with a focus on behavior at the interface of market and government, for over 20 years; scholarly studies published in the top journals including *The Journal of Urban Economics*, *Economic Inquiry* and *Land Economics*.

Randall W. Roth
Professor of Law
William S. Richardson School of Law
University of Hawaii

> Has taught at the University of Hawaii since 1982; tax counsel to Honolulu law firm Goodsill Anderson Quinn & Stifel since 1985; nationally recognized author on taxation and estate planning; former member of Hawaii State Tax Review Commission.

Marcia Y. Sakai
Assistant Professor
Business Administration and Economics Division
University of Hawaii at Hilo

B.A. and M.A. in mathematics and Ph.D. in economics from the University of Hawaii; consultant to Hawaii State Tax Review Commission; research focuses on tourism development and tax policy.

Michael A. Sklarz
Senior Vice President and Director of Research
Locations, Inc.

B.S. in applied mathematics, Columbia University; M.S. and Ph.D. in ocean engineering, University of Hawaii; author of the quarterly "Hawaii Real Estate Indicators" and numerous papers in academic journals; heads consulting division at Locations, Inc. working with developers, lenders and government agencies.

A.A. " Bud" Smyser
Contributing Editor
Honolulu Star-Bulletin

Writer and editor with the *Honolulu Star-Bulletin* since 1946; born and educated in Pennsylvania and first came to Hawaii as a naval officer on Pacific Fleet duty during World War II.

Jack P. Suyderhoud
Professor of Decision Sciences
College of Business Administration
University of Hawaii

Ph.D. in Economics, Purdue University; taught at the University of Hawaii College of Business Administration since 1978; Executive Director of the Hawaii State Tax Review Commission 1984-1985; has published numerous papers on state-local tax policy; consultant to the County of Hawaii, the State of Hawaii and the Government of Guam.

Bill Wood
Editor
Hawaii Investor Magazine

Business writer for 35 years, the last 20 based in Hawaii; has written for *The Wall Street Journal, Far Eastern Economic Review, Forbes, Newsweek* and other publications in the U.S., Europe and the Far East; founder-editor of *Hawaii Investor* magazine.

EMERGENCY POWER